The Progressive Era and the Great War
1896–1920

GOLDENTREE BIBLIOGRAPHIES

In American History
under the series editorship of
Arthur S. Link

The Progressive Era
and the Great War
1896–1920

compiled by

Arthur S. Link

Princeton University

and

William M. Leary, Jr.

San Diego State College

APPLETON-CENTURY-CROFTS

Educational Division

New York   MEREDITH CORPORATION

Editor's Foreword

GOLDENTREE BIBLIOGRAPHIES IN AMERICAN HISTORY are designed to provide students, teachers, and librarians with ready and reliable guides to the literature of American history in all its remarkable scope and variety. Volumes in the series cover comprehensively the major periods in American history, while additional volumes are devoted to all important subjects.

Goldentree Bibliographies attempt to steer a middle course between the brief list of references provided in the average textbook and the long bibliography in which significant items are often lost in the sheer number of titles listed. Each bibliography is, therefore, selective, with the sole criterion for choice being the significance—and not the age—of any particular work. The result is bibliographies of all works, including journal articles and doctoral dissertations, that are still useful, without bias in favor of any particular historiographical school.

Each compiler is a scholar long associated, both in research and teaching, with the period or subject of his volume. All compilers have not only striven to accomplish the objective of this series but have also cheerfully adhered to a general style and format. However, each compiler has been free to define his field, make his own selections, and work out internal organization as the unique demands of his period or subject have seemed to dictate.

The single great objective of *Goldentree Bibliographies in American History* will have been achieved if these volumes help researchers and students to find their way to the significant literature of American history.

Arthur S. Link

Preface

ANY BIBLIOGRAPHY THAT attempts to deal with the entire body of historical writing about the United States and its world relations during an important period is bound to be highly selective. This bibliography, covering the main developments in American history between 1896 and 1920, is no exception. However, we have tried to include most significant books and articles on American political history during this period, and also to list the more important works in other fields to which special bibliographies in the series will be devoted. In addition, we have cited selected doctoral dissertations, publications in foreign languages, memoirs, and collections of printed documents and other papers of special note. More extensive bibliographical information usually can be found in the appropriate secondary works.

We hope that the topical organization of this volume, combined with frequent cross-references, will facilitate its use.

Finally, we trust that students will learn as much from using this bibliography as we learned in compiling it.

A.S.L.

W.M.L., Jr.

Abbreviations

Ag Hist	Agricultural History
Am Econ Rev	American Economic Review
Am Hist Rev	American Historical Review
Am J Int Law	American Journal of International Law
Am Pol Sci Rev	American Political Science Review
Am Q	American Quarterly
Am Sch	American Scholar
Ann Am Acad Pol Soc Sci	Annals, American Academy of Political and Social Science
Ann Assn Am Geog	Annals, Association of American Geographers
Bus Hist Rev	Business History Review
Cath Hist Rev	Catholic Historical Review
Church Hist	Church History
For Aff	Foreign Affairs
His-Am Hist Rev	Hispanic-American Historical Review
Int Lab Rev	International Labour Review
J Am Hist	Journal of American History
J Am Stat Assn	Journal, American Statistical Association
J Econ Hist	Journal of Economic History
J Hist Ideas	Journal of the History of Ideas
J Mod Hist	Journal of Modern History
J Neg Hist	Journal of Negro History
J Pol	Journal of Politics
J Pol Econ	Journal of Political Economy
J Presby Hist	Journal of Presbyterian History
J S Hist	Journal of Southern History
Jour Q	Journalism Quarterly
Lab Hist	Labor History
Mid-Am	Mid-America
Miss Val Hist Rev	Mississippi Valley Historical Review
N Car Hist Rev	North Carolina Historical Review
N Eng Q	New England Quarterly
Neb Hist	Nebraska History
Pac Hist Rev	Pacific Historical Review
Pol Sci Q	Political Science Quarterly
Proc Acad Pol Sci	Proceedings, Academy of Political Science
Proc Am Philos Soc	Proceedings, American Philosophical Society
Pub Am Jew Hist Soc	Publications, American Jewish Historical Society
Pub Am Stat Assn	Publications, American Statistical Association
Pub Opin Q	Public Opinion Quarterly
Q J Econ	Quarterly Journal of Economics
Rec Am Cath Hist Soc	Records, American Catholic Historical Society
Rev Econ Stat	Review of Economic Statistics
Rev Pol	Review of Politics
S Atl Q	South Atlantic Quarterly
W Pol Q	Western Political Quarterly
Yale Rev	Yale Review

Note:
Cross-references are to page (**bold face**) and to item numbers (roman). Items marked by a dagger (†) are available in paperback edition at the time this bibliography goes to press. The publisher and compiler invite suggestions for additions to future editions of the bibliography.

Contents

Editor's Foreword   v
Preface   vii
Abbreviations   viii
I.   Bibliographical Guides and Selected Reference Works   1
II. American Politics from Theodore Roosevelt to Woodrow
     Wilson   2
     1. General   2
     2. Biographies, Autobiographies, and Collected Works   4
     3. The Progressive Movement   8
         A. GENERAL   8
         B. PROGRESSIVISM IN THE CITIES AND STATES   9
         C. THE SOCIAL JUSTICE MOVEMENT   12
         D. THE SOCIAL GOSPEL MOVEMENT   13
         E. THE MUCKRAKERS   14
         F. THE CONSERVATION MOVEMENT   14
         G. AGRARIAN MOVEMENTS   15
         H. INTELLECTUAL PROGRESSIVISM   15
     4. The Republican Era, 1901–1913   16
     5. The Wilson Era, 1913–1920   18
         A. GENERAL   18
         B. THE NEW FREEDOM   20
         C. THE FIRST WORLD WAR AND AFTER   22
     6. The Supreme Court   25
     7. Socialism   26
III. The United States and Its World Relations   27
     1. General   27
     2. Imperialism and the War with Spain   28
     3. The United States and Latin America   30
     4. The United States and Europe   32
     5. The United States and Asia   33
     6. The Road to War, 1914–1917   36
     7. The First World War, Versailles, and the Great
         Betrayal   39
IV. The American People and Their Economic Institutions   43
     1. General   43
     2. Demographic Changes   43

	3.	*Concentration, Competition, and Public Policy*	44
	4.	*Finance Capitalism*	45
	5.	*Manufacturing and Other Industries*	46
	6.	*Transportation*	48
	7.	*Agriculture*	49
	8.	*Research and Technology*	50
	9.	*Labor*	51
	10.	*Immigration*	54
V.		Social and Intellectual Main Currents in American Life	56
	1.	*Social Trends and Changes*	56
	2.	*Currents of American Thought*	57
	3.	*Education*	58
	4.	*Science, Medicine, and Public Health*	59
	5.	*Religion*	60
	6.	*The Arts*	61
	7.	*Journalism*	62
	8.	*The Negro*	63
	9.	*Nativism*	65
Notes			69
Index			75

I. Bibliographical Guides and Selected Reference Works

1 American Historical Association. *Guide to Historical Literature.* New York, 1961.

2 American Historical Association. *Writings on American History.* 46 vols. Washington, D.C., 1902–1964.

3 BASSETT, T. D. Seymour. "Bibliography: Descriptive and Critical." Vol. II of *Socialism and American Life.* Ed. by Donald D. Egbert and Stow Persons. 2 vols. Princeton, 1952.

4 BEMIS, Samuel Flagg and Grace Gardner GRIFFIN, eds. *Guide to the Diplomatic History of the United States, 1775–1921.* Washington, D.C., 1935.

5 Bureau of the Census. *Historical Statistics of the United States, Colonial Times to 1957.* Washington, D.C., 1960.

6 BURR, Nelson R. "A Critical Bibliography of Religion in America." Vols. III and IV of *Religion in American Life.* Ed. by James W. Smith and A. Leland Jamison. 4 vols. Princeton, 1961.

7 ELLIS, John Tracy. *A Guide to American Catholic History.* Milwaukee, 1959.

8 GRANTHAM, Dewey W., Jr. "Theodore Roosevelt in American Historical Writing, 1945–1960." *Mid-Am,* XLIV (1961), 3–35.

9 HANDLIN, Oscar, *et al. Harvard Guide to American History.* Cambridge, Mass., 1963.†

10 HIGHAM, John, ed. *The Reconstruction of American History.* New York, 1962.†

11 JOHNSON, Allen and Dumas MALONE, eds. *Dictionary of American Biography.* 22 vols. New York, 1928–1958.

12 KAPLAN, Louis, ed. *A Bibliography of American Autobiographies.* Madison, Wis., 1961.

13 KUEHL, Warren F., ed. *Dissertations in History: An Index to Dissertations Completed in History Departments of United States and Canadian Universities, 1873–1960.* Lexington, Ky., 1965.

14 LARSON, Henrietta M. *Guide to Business History.* Cambridge, Mass., 1948.

15 Library of Congress. *A Guide to the Study of the United States of America.* Washington, D.C., 1960.

16 LINK, Arthur S. and Rembert W. PATRICK, eds. *Writing Southern History: Essays in Historiography in Honor of Fletcher M. Green.* Baton Rouge, 1965.†

17 MAY, Ernest R. *American Intervention: 1917 and 1941.* Publication no. 30, Service Center for Teachers of History. Washington, D.C., 1960.

18 MILLER, Elizabeth W., ed. *The Negro in America: A Bibliography.* Cambridge, Mass., 1966.†

19 MORRIS, Richard B., ed. *Encyclopedia of American History.* Rev. ed. New York, 1961.

20 MOWRY, George E. *The Progressive Movement, 1900–1920: Recent Ideas and New Literature.* Publication no. 10, Service Center for Teachers of History. New York, 1958.

1   National Research Council , *et al. Doctoral Dissertations Accepted by American Universities. . . .* 22 vols. New York, 1933–1955.

2   NEUFELD, Maurice F. *A Representative Bibliography of American Labor History.* Ithaca, N.Y., 1964.

3   ROBERTS, Henry L., ed. *Foreign Affairs Bibliography: A Selected and Annotated List of Books on International Relations, 1952–1962.* New York, 1964.

4   SPILLER, Robert E., *et al.,* eds. *Literary History of the United States.* Rev. ed. New York, 1963.

5   STROUD, Gene S. and Gilbert E. DONAHUE. *Labor History in the United States: A General Bibliography.* Urbana, Ill., 1961.

6   WATSON, Richard L., Jr. "Woodrow Wilson and His Interpreters, 1947–1957." *Miss Val Hist Rev,* LXIV (1957), 207–236.

7   WOOLBERT, Robert Gale, ed. *Foreign Affairs Bibliography: A Selected and Annotated List of Books on International Relations, 1932–1942.* New York, 1945.

II. American Politics from Theodore Roosevelt to Woodrow Wilson

1. General

8   BLAISDELL, Thomas C., Jr. *The Federal Trade Commission: An Experiment in the Control of Business.* New York, 1932.

9   BRANDEIS, Elizabeth. "Labor Legislation." *History of Labor in the United States.* Ed. by John R. Commons, *et al.* 4 vols. New York, 1918–1935.

10   CHAMBERLAIN, John. *Farewell to Reform.* New York, 1932.†

11   CLARK, John Bates and John Maurice CLARK. *The Control of Trusts.* New York, 1914.

12   CLARK, John D. *The Federal Trust Policy.* Baltimore, 1931.

13   CUSHMAN, Robert E. "Social and Economic Controls through Federal Taxation." *Minnesota Law Review,* XVIII (1934), 759–783.

14   DORSETT, Lyle W. *The Pendergast Machine.* New York, 1968.

15   FAINSOD, Merle and Lincoln GORDON. *Government and the American Economy.* Rev. ed. New York, 1959.

16   FAULKNER, Harold U. *Politics, Reform, and Expansion, 1890–1900.* New York, 1958.†

17   FAULKNER, Harold U. *The Quest for Social Justice, 1898–1914.* New York, 1931.

18   FINE, Sidney. *Laissez Faire and the General Welfare State.* Ann Arbor, Mich., 1956.†

19   FRANKLIN, John Hope. *From Slavery to Freedom: A History of American Negroes.* Rev. ed. New York, 1956.

1 GINGER, Ray. *Age of Excess: The United States from 1877 to 1914.* New York, 1965.†

2 GREEN, Marguerite. *The National Civic Federation and the American Labor Movement, 1900–1925.* Washington, D.C., 1956.

3 HARBESON, Robert W. "Railroads and Regulation, 1877–1916: Conspiracy or Public Interest?" *J. Econ Hist,* XXVII (1967), 230-242.

4 HAYS, Samuel P. *The Response to Industrialism, 1885–1914.* Chicago, 1957.†

5 HAYS, Samuel P. "The Social Analysis of American Political History, 1880–1920." *Pol Sci Q,* LXXX (1965), 373-394.

6 HIGHAM, John. *Strangers in the Land: Patterns of American Nativism, 1860–1925.* New Brunswick, N.J., 1955.†

7 HOFSTADTER, Richard. *Age of Reform.* New York, 1955.†

8 HOLLINGSWORTH, J. Rogers. *The Whirligig of Politics: The Democracy of Cleveland and Bryan.* Chicago, 1964.

9 KARSON, Marc. *American Labor Unions and Politics, 1900–1918.* Carbondale, Ill., 1958.

10 KOLKO, Gabriel. *Railroads and Regulation.* Princeton, 1965.

11 KOLKO, Gabriel. *The Triumph of Conservatism.* New York, 1963.

12 LESCOHIER, Don D. "Working Conditions." *History of Labor in the United States.* Ed. by John R. Commons, *et al.* See **2.9.**

13 LINK, Arthur S., *et al. American Epoch: A History of the United States Since the 1890's.* 3rd ed. New York, 1967.†

14 MILLS, Frederick C. *Economic Tendencies in the United States: Aspects of Pre-War and Post-War Changes.* New York, 1932.

15 MITCHELL, Wesley C. *Business Cycles and Their Causes.* Berkeley, 1941.†

16 PERLMAN, Selig and Philip TAFT. "Labor Movements, 1896–1932." *History of Labor in the United States.* Ed. by John R. Commons, *et al.* See **2.9.**

17 RATNER, Sidney. *American Taxation.* New York, 1942.

18 SEAGER, Henry R. and Charles A. GULICK. *Trust and Corporation Problems.* New York, 1929.

19 SHARFMAN, I. L. *The Interstate Commerce Commission: A Study in Administrative Law and Procedure.* 4 vols. New York, 1931–1937.

20 SULLIVAN, Mark. *Our Times, 1900–1925.* 6 vols. New York, 1927–1935.

21 TAUSSIG, Frank W. *Tariff History of the United States.* 8th ed. New York, 1931.†

22 THORELLI, Hans B. *The Federal Antitrust Policy.* Stockholm, 1954.

23 TINDALL, George Brown. *The Emergence of the New South, 1913–1945.* Baton Rouge, 1967.

24 WATKINS, Myron W. *Industrial Combinations and Public Policy.* Boston, 1957.

25 WIEBE, Robert H. *The Search for Order, 1877–1920.* New York, 1967.

2. Biographies, Autobiographies, and Collected Works

1 ADDAMS, Jane. *The Second Twenty Years at Hull-House.* New York, 1930.

2 ADDAMS, Jane. *Twenty Years at Hull-House.* New York, 1910.†

3 BAKER, Ray Stannard. *American Chronicle.* New York, 1945.

4 BAKER, Ray Stannard. *Woodrow Wilson: Life and Letters.* 8 vols. Garden City, N.Y., 1927–1939.

5 BAKER, Ray Stannard and William E. DODD, eds. *The Public Papers of Woodrow Wilson.* 6 vols. New York, 1925–1927.

6 BANNISTER, Robert C., Jr. *Ray Stannard Baker: The Mind and Thought of a Progressive.* New Haven, 1966.

7 BARKER, Charles A. *Henry George.* New York, 1955.

8 BELL, Herbert C. F. *Woodrow Wilson and the People.* Garden City, N.Y., 1945.

9 BILLINGTON, Monroe Lee. *Thomas P. Gore.* Lawrence, Kan., 1967.

10 BLUM, John M. *Joe Tumulty and the Wilson Era.* Boston, 1951.

11 BLUM, John M. *Woodrow Wilson and the Politics of Morality.* Boston, 1956.†

12 BLUMBERG, Dorothy Rose. *Florence Kelley: The Making of a Social Pioneer.* New York, 1966.

13 BOWERS, Claude G. *Beveridge and the Progressive Era.* New York, 1932.

14 BRAGDON, Henry W. *Woodrow Wilson: The Academic Years.* Cambridge, Mass., 1967.

15 BRODERICK, Francis L. *W. E. B. Du Bois: Negro Leader in a Time of Crisis.* Stanford, 1959.†

16 BROOKS, Aubrey L. and Hugh T. LEFLER, eds. *The Papers of Walter Clark.* 2 vols. Chapel Hill, 1948–1949.

17 BRYAN, Mary B., ed. *The Memoirs of William Jennings Bryan.* Philadelphia, 1925.

18 BUTT, Archibald W. *Taft and Roosevelt: The Intimate Letters of Archie Butt, Military Aide.* 2 vols. Garden City, N.Y., 1930.

19 COBEN, Stanley. *A. Mitchell Palmer: Politician.* New York, 1963.

20 COIT, Margaret L. *Mr. Baruch.* Boston, 1957.

21 COLETTA, Paola E. *William Jennings Bryan: Political Evangelist, 1860–1908.* Lincoln, Neb., 1964.

22 COMMONS, John R. *Myself.* New York, 1934.†

23 CRAMER, Clarence H. *Newton D. Baker.* Cleveland, 1961.

24 CREEL, George. *Rebel at Large.* New York, 1947.

1   CROLY, Herbert D. *Marcus Alonzo Hanna.* New York, 1912.

2   CRONON, E. David, ed. *The Cabinet Diaries of Josephus Daniels, 1913–1921.* Lincoln, Neb., 1963.

3   DANIELS, Josephus. *Editor in Politics.* Chapel Hill, 1941.

4   DANIELS, Josephus. *Tar Heel Editor.* Chapel Hill, 1939.

5   DANIELS, Josephus. *The Wilson Era.* 2 vols. Chapel Hill, 1944–1946.

6   ELLIS, Elmer. *Mr. Dooley's America: A Life of Finley Peter Dunne.* New York, 1941.

7   ELY, Richard T. *Ground Under Our Feet.* New York, 1938.

8   FOWLER, Dorothy. *John Coit Spooner.* New York, 1961.

9   FREIDEL, Frank. *Franklin D. Roosevelt: The Apprenticeship.* Boston, 1952.

10 GARRATY, John A. *Henry Cabot Lodge.* New York, 1953.

11 GARRATY, John A. *Right-Hand Man: The Life of George W. Perkins.* New York, 1960.

12 GARRATY, John A. *Woodrow Wilson.* New York, 1956.

13 GARRATY, John A. "Woodrow Wilson: A Study in Personality." *S Atl Q,* LVI (1957), 176-185.

14 GEIGER, Louis G. *Joseph W. Folk of Missouri.* Columbia, Mo., 1953.

15 GEORGE, Alexander L. and Juliette L. *Woodrow Wilson and Colonel House: A Personality Study.* New York, 1956.†

16 GINGER, Ray. *The Bending Cross: A Biography of Eugene Victor Debs.* New Brunswick, N.J., 1949.†

17 GLAD, Paul W. *The Trumpet Soundeth: William Jennings Bryan and His Democracy, 1896–1912.* Lincoln, Neb., 1960.†

18 GOLDMARK, Josephine C. *Impatient Crusader: Florence Kelley's Life Story.* Urbana, Ill., 1953.

19 GOMPERS, Samuel. *Seventy Years of Life and Labor: An Autobiography.* 2 vols. New York, 1925.

20 GOTTFRIED, Alex. *Boss Cermak of Chicago.* Seattle, 1962.

21 GRANTHAM, Dewey W., Jr. *Hoke Smith and the Politics of the New South.* Baton Rouge, 1958.†

22 GRAYSON, Cary T. *Woodrow Wilson: An Intimate Memoir.* New York, 1960.

23 GWINN, William Rea. *Uncle Joe Cannon, Archfoe of Insurgency.* New York, 1957.

24 HAGEDORN, Hermann. *Leonard Wood.* 2 vols. New York, 1931.

25 HAGEDORN, Hermann. *The Roosevelt Family of Sagamore Hill.* New York, 1954.

1 HARBAUGH, William H. *Power and Responsibility: The Life and Times of Theodore Roosevelt.* New York, 1961.†

2 HELMES, Winifred G. *John A. Johnson, the People's Governor.* Minneapolis, 1949.

3 HENDRICK, Burton J. *The Life of Andrew Carnegie.* 2 vols. New York, 1932.

4 HENDRICK, Burton J. *The Life and Letters of Walter H. Page.* 3 vols. Garden City, N.Y., 1922–1925.

5 HOUSTON, David F. *Eight Years with Wilson's Cabinet, 1913 to 1920.* 2 vols. Garden City, N.Y., 1926.

6 HOWE, Frederic C. *The Confessions of a Reformer.* New York, 1925.†

7 HOWE, M. A. DeWolfe. *George von Lengerke Meyer.* New York, 1920.

8 HUTCHINSON, William T. *Lowden of Illinois.* 2 vols. Chicago, 1957.

9 HUTHMACHER, J. Joseph. *Senator Robert F. Wagner and the Rise of Urban Liberalism.* New York, 1968.

10 JESSUP, Philip C. *Elihu Root.* 2 vols. New York, 1938.

11 JOHNSON, Tom L. *My Story.* New York, 1911.

12 JOHNSON, Walter. *William Allen White's America.* New York, 1947.

13 KERNEY, James. *The Political Education of Woodrow Wilson.* New York, 1926.

14 LA FOLLETTE, Belle C. and Fola. *Robert M. La Follette.* 2 vols. New York, 1953.

15 LAMBERT, John R. *Arthur Pue Gorman.* Baton Rouge, 1953.

16 LAMBERT, Oscar D. *Stephen Benton Elkins.* Pittsburgh, 1955.

17 LANE, Anne W. and Louise H. WALL, eds. *The Letters of Franklin K. Lane, Personal and Political.* Boston, 1922.

18 LARSEN, William. *Montague of Virginia: The Making of a Southern Progressive.* Baton Rouge, 1965.

19 LEOPOLD, Richard W. *Elihu Root and the Conservative Tradition.* Boston, 1954.†

20 LEVINE, Lawrence W. *Defender of the Faith: William Jennings Bryan; the Last Decade, 1915–1925.* New York, 1965.

21 LINK, Arthur S., *et al.,* eds. *The Papers of Woodrow Wilson.* 5 vols. to date. Princeton, 1966–

22 LINK, Arthur S. *Wilson: Campaigns for Progressivism and Peace, 1916–1917.* Princeton, 1965.

23 LINK, Arthur S. *Wilson: Confusions and Crises, 1915–1916.* Princeton, 1964.

24 LINK, Arthur S. *Wilson: The New Freedom.* Princeton, 1956.†

25 LINK, Arthur S. *Wilson: The Road to the White House.* Princeton, 1947.†

26 LINK, Arthur S. *Wilson: The Struggle for Neutrality, 1914–1915.* Princeton, 1960.

27 LINK, Arthur S. *Woodrow Wilson: A Brief Biography.* Cleveland, 1963.

28 LINN, James Weber. *Jane Addams.* New York, 1935.

1   LOWITT, Richard. *George W. Norris: The Making of a Progressive, 1861–1912.* Syracuse, 1963.

2   MANDEL, Bernard. *Samuel Gompers: A Biography.* Yellow Springs, Ohio, 1963.

3   MANN, Arthur. *La Guardia: A Fighter Against his Times, 1882–1933.* Philadelphia, 1959.

4   MASON, Alpheus T. *Brandeis: A Free Man's Life.* New York, 1946.

5   MAXWELL, Robert S. *Emanuel L. Philipp: Wisconsin Stalwart.* Madison, Wis., 1959.

6   MC ADOO, William G. *Crowded Years: The Reminiscences of William G. McAdoo.* Boston, 1931.

7   MC GEARY, M. Nelson. *Gifford Pinchot, Forester-Politician.* Princeton, 1960.

8   MORISON, Elting E. *Turmoil and Tradition: A Study of the Life and Times of Henry L. Stimson.* Boston, 1960.†

9   MORISON, Elting E. and John M. BLUM, eds. *The Letters of Theodore Roosevelt.* 8 vols. Cambridge, Mass., 1951–1954.

10 NEVINS, Allan. *The Letters and Journal of Brand Whitlock.* 2 vols. New York, 1936.

11 NORRIS, George W. *Fighting Liberal: The Autobiography of George W. Norris.* New York, 1945.†

12 OLDER, Fremont. *William Randolph Hearst.* New York, 1936.

13 ORR, Oliver H., Jr. *Charles Brantley Aycock.* Chapel Hill, 1961.

14 OSBORN, George C. *John Sharp Williams.* Baton Rouge, 1943.

15 PALMER, Frederick. *Newton D. Baker.* 2 vols. New York, 1931.

16 PERKINS, Dexter. *Charles Evans Hughes and American Democratic Statesmanship.* Boston, 1956.†

17 PRINGLE, Henry F. *The Life and Times of William Howard Taft.* 2 vols. New York, 1939.

18 PRINGLE, Henry F. *Theodore Roosevelt.* New York, 1931.†

19 PUSEY, Merlo J. *Charles Evans Hughes.* 2 vols. New York, 1951.

20 ROOSEVELT, Theodore. *An Autobiography.* New York, 1919.

21 *The Works of Theodore Roosevelt.* 20 vols. (National edition.) New York, 1926.

22 ROPER, Daniel C. *Fifty Years of Public Life.* Durham, N.C., 1941.

23 ROSS, Edward A. *Seventy Years of It.* New York, 1936.

24 SAGE, Leland L. *William Boyd Allison: A Study in Practical Politics.* Iowa City, 1956.

25 SEYMOUR, Charles. *The Intimate Papers of Colonel House.* 4 vols. Boston, 1926–1928.

26 SIMKINS, Francis B. *Pitchfork Ben Tillman, South Carolinian.* Baton Rouge, 1944.†

27 SMITH, Rixey and Norman BEASLEY. *Carter Glass.* New York, 1939.

1   STEFFENS, Lincoln. *The Autobiography of Lincoln Steffens.* New York, 1931.†

2   STEPHENSON, George M. *John Lind of Minnesota.* Minneapolis, 1935.

3   STEPHENSON, Nathaniel W. *Nelson W. Aldrich.* New York, 1930.

4   SULLIVAN, Mark. *The Education of an American.* New York, 1938.

5   SWANBERG, W. A. *Citizen Hearst.* New York, 1961.†

6   SWANBERG, W. A. *Pulitzer.* New York, 1967.

7   VANCE, Maurice M. *Charles Richard Van Hise: Scientist Progressive.* Madison, Wis., 1960.

8   VILLARD, Osward Garrison. *Fighting Years: Memoirs of a Liberal Editor.* New York, 1939.

9   WADE, Louise C. *Graham Taylor: Pioneer for Social Justice, 1851–1938.* Chicago, 1964.

10   WALD, Lillian D. *The House on Henry Street.* New York, 1915.

11   WALWORTH, Arthur. *Woodrow Wilson.* 2 vols. New York, 1958.

12   WASHINGTON, Booker T. *Up From Slavery.* New York, 1901.†

13   WATTERSON, Henry. *"Marse Henry:" An Autobiography.* 2 vols. New York, 1919.

14   WHITE, William Allen. *The Autobiography of William Allen White.* New York, 1946.

15   WINTER, Ella and Granville HICKS, eds. *The Letters of Lincoln Steffens.* 2 vols. New York, 1938.

16   WOODWARD, C. Vann. *Tom Watson, Agrarian Rebel.* New York, 1938.†

17   ZUCKER, Norman L. *George W. Norris: Gentle Knight of American Democracy.* Urbana, Ill., 1966.

3. The Progressive Movement

A. GENERAL

18   ALLEN, Howard W. "Geography and Politics: Voting on Reform Issues in the United States Senate, 1911–1916." *J S Hist,* XXVII (1961), 216-228.

19   BOWERS, Claude G. *Beveridge and the Progressive Era.* See 4.13.

20   BRAEMAN, John. "Seven Progressives." *Bus Hist Rev,* XXXV (1961), 581-592.

21   BROOKS, Aubrey L. and Hugh T. LEFLER, eds. *The Papers of Walter Clark.* See 4.16.

22   BRYAN, Mary B., ed. *The Memoirs of William Jennings Bryan.* See 4.17.

23   CHAMBERLAIN, John. *Farewell to Reform.* See 2.10.

24   COLETTA, Paola E. *William Jennings Bryan.* See 4.21.

25   CUTLIP, Scott M. *Fund Raising in the United States: Its Role in America's Philanthropy.* New Brunswick, N.J., 1965.

26   DANIELS, Josephus. *Editor in Politics.* See 5.3.

1 DANIELS, Josephus. *Tar Heel Editor.* See **5.4.**

2 DE WITT, Benjamin Parke. *The Progressive Movement.* New York, 1915.

3 ELY, Richard T. *Ground Under Our Feet.* See **5.7.**

4 FLEXNER, Eleanor. *Century of Struggle: The Woman's Rights Movement in the United States.* Cambridge, Mass., 1959.

5 GLAD, Paul W. *The Trumpet Soundeth.* See **5.17.**

6 GRANTHAM, Dewey W., Jr. "The Progressive Era and the Reform Tradition." *Mid-Am,* XLVI (1964), 227-251.

7 HABER, Samuel. *Efficiency and Uplift: Scientific Management in the Progressive Era, 1890–1920.* Chicago, 1964.

8 HILLJE, John W. "The Progressive Movement and the Graduated Income Tax, 1913–1919." Doctoral dissertation, University of Texas, 1966.

9 HOFSTADTER, Richard. *Age of Reform.* See **3.7**

10 HOWE, Frederic C. *The Confessions of a Reformer.* See **6.6.**

11 JACK, Robert L. *History of the National Association for the Advancement of Colored People.* Boston, 1943.

12 KELLOGG, Charles Flint. *NAACP: A History of the National Association for the Advancement of Colored People, 1909–1920.* Baltimore, 1967.

13 KELLOGG, Paul Underwood, ed. *The Pittsburgh Survey.* 6 vols. New York, 1909–1914.

14 KOLKO, Gabriel. *The Triumph of Conservatism.* See **3.11.**

15 KRADITOR, Aileen S. *The Ideas of the Woman Suffrage Movement, 1890–1920.* New York, 1965.

16 LEVINE, Daniel. *Varieties of Reform Thought.* Madison, Wis., 1964.

17 MADISON, Charles A. *Leaders and Liberals in 20th Century America.* New York, 1961.

18 MASON, Alpheus T. *Brandeis.* See **7.4.**

19 ODEGARD, Peter H. *Pressure Politics: The Story of the Anti-Saloon League.* New York, 1928.

20 TAGER, Jack. "Progressives, Conservatives, and the Theory of Status Revolution." *Mid-Am,* XLVIII (1966), 162-175.

21 TIMBERLAKE, James H. *Prohibition and the Progressive Movement, 1900–1920.* Cambridge, Mass., 1963.

22 WIEBE, Robert H. *Businessmen and Reform: A Study of the Progressive Movement.* Cambridge, Mass., 1962.

B. PROGRESSIVISM IN THE CITIES AND STATES

23 ABRAMS, Richard M. *Conservatism in a Progressive Era: Massachusetts Politics, 1900–1912.* Cambridge, Mass., 1964.

24 ABRAMS, Richard M. "A Paradox of Progressivism: Massachusetts on the Eve of Insurgency." *Pol Sci Q,* LXXV (1960), 379-399.

25 BACON, Charles Reade. *A People Awakened.* Garden City, N.Y., 1912.

26 CROOKS, James B. *Politics and Progress: The Rise of Urban Progressivism in Baltimore, 1895–1911.* Baton Rouge, 1968.

1   BEAN, Walton E. *Boss Ruef's San Francisco.* Berkeley, 1952.†

2   DOHERTY, Herbert J., Jr. "Voices of Protest from the New South, 1875–1910." *Miss Val Hist Rev,* XLII (1955), 45-66.

3   FERRELL, Henry C., Jr. "Prohibition, Reform, and Politics in Virginia, 1895–1916." *East Carolina College Publications in History,* III (1966), 175-242.

4   FLINT, Winston Allen. *The Progressive Movement in Vermont.* Washington, D. C., 1941.

5   GEIGER, Louis G. *Joseph W. Folk of Missouri.* See **5.14.**

6   GIST, Genevieve B. "Progressive Reform in a Rural Community: The Adams County [Ohio] Vote-Fraud Case." *Miss Val Hist Rev,* XLVIII (1961), 60-78.

7   GLAAB, Charles N. "The Failure of North Dakota Progressivism." *Mid-Am,* XXXIX (1957), 195-209.

8   GOTTFRIED, Alex. *Boss Cermak of Chicago.* See **5.20.**

9   GRANTHAM, Dewey W., Jr. *Hoke Smith and the Politics of the New South.* See **5.21.**

10   GREEN, Constance. *Washington: Capital City, 1879–1950.* Princeton, 1953.

11   GREEN, Fletcher M. "Some Aspects of the Convict Lease System in the Southern States." *Essays in Southern History Presented to Joseph Gregoire de Roulhac Hamilton. . . .* Ed. by Fletcher M. Green. Chapel Hill, 1949.

12   HACKNEY, Sheldon. "From Populism to Progressivism in Alabama, 1890–1910." Doctoral dissertation, Yale University, 1966.

13   HAYS, Samuel P. "The Politics of Reform in Municipal Government in the Progressive Era." *Pacific Northwest Quarterly,* LV (1964), 157-169.

14   HELMES, Winifred G. *John A. Johnson, the People's Governor.* See **6.2.**

15   HIRST, David W., ed. *Woodrow Wilson: Reform Governor.* Princeton, 1965.

16   HUTHMACHER, J. Joseph. *Senator Robert F. Wagner and the Rise of Urban Liberalism.* See **6.9.**

17   HUTHMACHER, J. Joseph. "Urban Liberalism and the Age of Reform." *Miss Val Hist Rev,* XLIX (1962), 231-241.

18   ISAAC, Paul E. *Prohibition and Politics: Turbulent Decades in Tennessee, 1885–1920.* Knoxville, 1965.

19   JOHNSON, Tom L. *My Story.* See **6.11.**

20   KERR, William T., Jr. "The Progressives in Washington, 1910–1912." *Pacific Northwest Quarterly,* LV (1964), 16-27.

21   KIRWAN, Albert D. *The Revolt of the Rednecks: Mississippi Politics, 1876–1925.* Lexington, Ky., 1951.†

22   LARSEN, William. *Montague of Virginia.* See **6.18.**

23   LINK, Arthur S. "The Progressive Movement in the South, 1870–1914." *N Car Hist Rev,* XXIII (1946), 172-195.

24   LOWITT, Richard. *George W. Norris.* See **7.1.**

1   MANN, Arthur. *Yankee Reformers in the Urban Era.* Cambridge, Mass., 1954.†

2   MAXWELL, Robert S. *Emanuel L. Philipp.* See 7.5.

3   MAXWELL, Robert S. *La Follette and the Rise of Progressives in Wisconsin.* Madison, Wis., 1956.

4   MC KELVEY, Blake. *Rochester: The Quest for Quality, 1890–1925.* Cambridge, Mass., 1956.

5   MILLER, William D. *Memphis during the Progressive Era, 1900–1917.* Memphis, 1957.

6   MILLER, Zane L. *Boss Cox's Cincinnati: Urban Politics in the Progressive Era.* New York, 1968.

7   MOWRY, George E. "The California Progressive and His Rationale: A Study in Middle Class Politics." *Miss Val Hist Rev,* XXXVI (1949), 239-250.

8   MOWRY, George E. *The California Progressives.* Berkeley, 1951.†

9   NOBLE, Ransom E., Jr. *New Jersey Progressivism Before Wilson.* Princeton, 1946.

10 NORRIS, George W. *Fighting Liberal.* See 7.11.

11 NYE, Russel B. *Midwestern Progressive Politics.* East Lansing, Mich., 1951.†

12 ORR, Oliver H., Jr. *Charles Brantley Aycock.* See 7.13.

13 OSBORN, George C. *John Sharp Williams.* See 7.14.

14 OSTRANDER, Gilman Marston. *The Prohibition Movement in California, 1848–1933.* Berkeley, 1957.

15 POTTS, E. Daniel. "The Progressive Profile in Iowa." *Mid-Am,* XLVII (1965), 257-268.

16 PUSEY, Merlo J. *Charles Evans Hughes.* See 7.19.

17 REYNOLDS, George M. *Machine Politics in New Orleans, 1897–1926.* New York, 1936.

18 SAXTON, Alexander. "San Francisco Labor and the Populist and Progressive Insurgencies." *Pac Hist Rev,* XXXIV (1965), 421-438.

19 SELLERS, James Benson. *The Prohibition Movement in Alabama, 1702 to 1943.* Chapel Hill, 1943.†

20 SHERMAN, Richard B. "The Status Revolution and Massachusetts Progressive Leadership." *Pol Sci Q,* LXXVIII (1963), 59-65.

21 STAPLES, Henry L. and Alpheus T. MASON. *The Fall of a Railroad Empire: Brandeis and the New Haven Merger Battle.* Syracuse, 1947.

22 STEELMAN, Joseph F. "The Progressive Era in North Carolina, 1884–1917." Doctoral dissertation, University of North Carolina, 1955.

23 STEELMAN, Joseph F. "Progressivism and Agitation for Legal Reform in North Carolina, 1897–1917." *East Carolina College Publications in History,* I (1964), 94-164.

24 STEFFENS, Lincoln. *The Shame of the Cities.* New York, 1904.†

25 STEFFENS, Lincoln. *The Struggle for Self-Government.* New York, 1906.

26 STEPHENSON, George M. *John Lind of Minnesota.* See 8.2.

27 STEWART, Frank M. *A Half-Century of Municipal Reform: The History of the National Municipal League.* Berkeley, 1950.

1 TAYLOR, A. Elizabeth. *The Woman Suffrage Movement in Tennessee.* New York, 1957.

2 THELEN, David P. "The Social and Political Origins of Wisconsin Progressivism, 1885–1900." Doctoral dissertation, University of Wisconsin, 1967.

3 TINSLEY, James A. "The Progressive Movement in Texas." Doctoral dissertation, University of Wisconsin, 1954.

4 WARNER, Hoyt Landon. *Progressivism in Ohio, 1897–1917.* Columbus Ohio, 1964.

5 WEINSTEIN, James. "Organized Business and the City Commission and Manager Movements." *J S Hist,* XXVIII (1962), 166-182.

6 WESSER, Robert F. *Charles Evans Hughes: Politics and Reform in New York, 1905–1910.* Ithaca, N.Y., 1967.

7 WHITENER, Daniel Jay. *Prohibition in North Carolina, 1715–1945.* Chapel Hill, 1946.

8 WOODWARD, C. Vann. *Origins of the New South, 1877–1913.* Baton Rouge, 1951.†

9 YELLOWITZ, Irwin. *Labor and the Progressive Movement in New York State, 1897–1916.* Ithaca, N.Y., 1965.

10 ZINK, Harold. *City Bosses in the United States.* Durham, N.C., 1930.

11 ZUCKER, Norman L. *George W. Norris.* See **8.17**.

C. THE SOCIAL JUSTICE MOVEMENT

12 ADDAMS, Jane. *The Second Twenty Years at Hull-House.* See **4.1**.

13 ADDAMS, Jane. *Twenty Years at Hull-House.* See **4.2**.

14 BLUMBERG, Dorothy Rose. *Florence Kelley.* See **4.12**.

15 BREMNER, Robert H. *American Philanthropy.* Chicago, 1960.†

16 BREMNER, Robert H. "The Big Flat: History of a New York Tenement House." *Am Hist Rev,* LXIV (1958), 54-62.

17 BREMNER, Robert H. *From the Depths: The Discovery of Poverty in the United States.* New York, 1956.†

18 BRUNO, Frank, Jr. and Louis TOWLEY. *Trends in Social Work, 1874–1956.* New York, 1957.

19 CHAMBERS, Clarke A. *Seedtime of Reform: American Social Service and Social Action, 1918–1933.* Minneapolis, 1963.

20 DAVIDSON, Elizabeth H. *Child Labor Legislation in the Southern Textile States.* Chapel Hill, 1939.

21 DAVIS, Allen F. "Settlement Workers in Politics, 1890–1914." *Rev Pol,* XXVI (1964), 505-517.

22 DAVIS, Allen F. "The Social Workers and the Progressive Party, 1912–1916." *Am Hist Rev,* LXIX (1964), 671-688.

23 DAVIS, Allen F. *Spearheads for Reform: The Social Settlements and the Progressive Movement, 1890–1914.* New York, 1967.

1 DERBER, Milton. "The Idea of Industrial Democracy in America, 1898–1915." *Lab Hist,* VII (1966), 259-286.

2 EASTMAN, Crystal. *Work-Accidents and the Law.* New York, 1910.

3 FELT, Jeremy P. *Hostages of Fortune: Child Labor Reform in New York State.* Syracuse, 1965.

4 GOLDMARK, Josephine C. *Impatient Crusader.* See 5.18.

5 GREER, Thomas H. *American Social Reform Movements: Their Pattern Since 1865.* New York, 1949.

6 HOLDEN, Arthur C. *The Settlement Idea.* New York, 1922.

7 HOWE, Frederic C. *The Confessions of a Reformer.* See 6.6.

8 LEVINE, Daniel. "Jane Addams: Romantic Radical, 1889–1912." *Mid-Am,* XLIV (1962), 195-210.

9 LINN, James Weber. *Jane Addams.* See 6.28.

10 LUBOVE, Roy. "Lawrence Veiller and the New York State Tenement House Commission of 1900." *Miss Val Hist Rev,* XLVII (1961), 659-677.

11 LUBOVE, Roy. *The Professional Altruist: The Emergence of Social Work as a Career, 1880–1930.* Cambridge, Mass., 1965.

12 LUBOVE, Roy. "The Progressives and the Prostitute." *Historian,* XXIV (1962), 308-330.

13 LUBOVE, Roy. *The Progressives and the Slums: Tenement House Reform in New York City, 1890–1917.* Pittsburgh, 1962.

14 LUBOVE, Roy. *The Struggle for Social Security, 1900–1935.* Cambridge, Mass., 1968.

15 LUBOVE, Roy. "The Twentieth Century City: The Progressive as Municipal Reformer." *Mid-Am,* XLI (1959), 195-209.

16 ROSS, Edward A. *Seventy Years of It.* See 7.23.

17 STEELMAN, Lala Carr. "Mary Clare de Graffenried: The Saga of a Crusader for Social Reform." *East Carolina College Publications in History,* III (1966), 53-84.

18 WADE, Louise C. *Graham Taylor.* See 8.9.

19 WALD, Lillian D. *The House on Henry Street.* See 8.10.

20 WEISS, Nancy Joan. *Charles Francis Murphy, 1858–1924: Respectability and Responsibility in Tammany Politics.* Northampton, Mass., 1968.

21 WOOD, Stephen B. *Constitutional Politics in the Progressive Era.* Chicago, 1967. (A study of the constitutional aspects of the campaign to establish federal child labor legislation.)

22 WOODS, Robert A. and Albert J. KENNEDY. *The Settlement Horizon: A National Estimate.* New York, 1922.

23 ZIMMERMAN, Jane. "The Penal Reform Movement in the South during the Progressive Era, 1890–1917." *J S Hist,* XVII (1951), 462-492.

D. THE SOCIAL GOSPEL MOVEMENT

24 ABELL, Aaron I. *American Catholicism and Social Action.* Garden City, N.Y., 1960.†

25 ABELL, Aaron I. *The Urban Impact on American Protestantism, 1865–1900.* Cambridge, Mass., 1943.

26 BARKER, John Marshall. *The Social Gospel and the New Era.* New York, 1919.

1   HOPKINS, Charles Howard. *The Rise of the Social Gospel in American Protestantism, 1865–1915.* New Haven, 1940.

2   MAY, Henry F. *Protestant Churches and Industrial America.* New York, 1949.

3   MILLER, Robert Moats. "Methodism and American Society, 1900–1939." *The History of American Methodism.* Ed. by Emory Stevens Bucke, *et al.* 3 vols. New York, 1964. Vol. III, 328-406.

4   MULLER, Dorothea R. "The Social Philosophy of Josiah Strong: Social Christianity and American Progressivism." *Church Hist,* XXVIII (1959), 183-201.

5   RAUSCHENBUSCH, Walter. *Christianity and the Social Crisis.* New York, 1907.†

6   RAUSCHENBUSCH, Walter. *A Theology for the Social Gospel.* New York, 1918.

7   SAPPINGTON, Roger E. *Brethren Social Policy, 1908–1958.* Elgin, Ill., 1961.

8   SMITH, Willard H. "William Jennings Bryan and the Social Gospel." *J Am Hist,* LIII (1966), 41-60.

9   STELZLE, Charles. *American Social and Religious Conditions.* New York, 1912.

E. THE MUCKRAKERS

10   CHALMERS, David Mark. *The Social and Political Ideas of the Muckrakers.* New York, 1964.†

11   FILLER, Louis. *Crusaders for American Liberalism.* New York, 1939.†

12   LYON, Peter. *Success Story: The Life and Times of S. S. McClure.* New York, 1963.

13   MOTT, Frank L. *American Journalism: A History, 1690–1960.* 3rd ed. New York, 1962.

14   MOTT, Frank L. *A History of American Magazines.* 4 vols. New York, 1930–1957.

15   REGIER, Cornelius C. *The Era of the Muckrakers.* Chapel Hill, 1932.

16   SCHULTZ, Stanley K. "The Morality of Politics: The Muckrakers' Vision of Democracy." *J Am Hist,* LII (1965), 527-547.

17   SINCLAIR, Upton. *Autobiography.* New York, 1962.

18   STEFFENS, Lincoln. *The Autobiography of Lincoln Steffens.* See 8.1.

19   WINTER, Ella and Granville HICKS, eds. *The Letters of Lincoln Steffens.* See 8.15.

F. THE CONSERVATION MOVEMENT

20   BATES, J. Leonard. "Fulfilling American Democracy: The Conservation Movement, 1907 to 1921." *Miss Val Hist Rev,* XLIV (1957), 29-57.

21   BATES, J. Leonard. *The Origins of Teapot Dome: Progressives, Parties, and Petroleum, 1909–1921.* Urbana, Ill., 1963.

22   CROSS, Whitney R. "Ideas in Politics: The Conservation Policies of the Two Roosevelts." *J Hist Ideas,* XIV (1953), 421-438.

1 DARLING, Arthur B., ed. *The Public Papers of Francis G. Newlands.* 2 vols. Boston, 1932.

2 HAYS, Samuel P. *Conservation and the Gospel of Efficiency: The Progressive Conservation Movement, 1890–1920.* Cambridge, Mass., 1959.

3 KING, Judson. *The Conservation Fight: From Theodore Roosevelt to the Tennessee Valley Authority.* Washington, D. C., 1945.

4 LOWITT, Richard. "A Neglected Aspect of the Progressive Movement: George W. Norris and Public Control of Hydro-Electric Power, 1913–1919." *Historian,* XXVII (1965), 350-365.

5 MC GEARY, M. Nelson. *Gifford Pinchot, Forester-Politician.* See 7.7.

6 PEFFER, E. Louise. *The Closing of the Public Domain: Disposal and Reservation Policies, 1900–1950.* Stanford, 1951.

7 PENICK, James, Jr. *Progressive Politics and Conservation: The Ballinger– Pinchot Affair.* Chicago, 1968.

8 RICHARDSON, Elmo R. *The Politics of Conservation: Crusaders and Controversies, 1897–1913.* Berkeley, 1962.

9 ROBBINS, Roy M. *Our Landed Heritage: The Public Domain, 1776–1936.* Princeton, 1942.†

G. AGRARIAN MOVEMENTS

10 FITE, Gilbert C. "Peter Norbeck and the Defeat of the Nonpartisan League in South Dakota." *Miss Val Hist Rev,* XXXIII (1946), 217-236.

11 JAMIESON, Stuart. *Labor Unionism in American Agriculture.* Washington, D. C., 1945.

12 MORLAN, Robert L. *Political Prairie Fire: The Nonpartisan League, 1915–1922.* Minneapolis, 1955.

13 SALOUTOS, Theodore. *Farmer Movements in the South, 1865–1933.* Berkeley, 1960.

14 SALOUTOS, Theodore. "The Rise of the Nonpartisan League in North Dakota, 1915–1917." *Ag Hist,* XX (1946), 43-61.

15 SALOUTOS, Theodore. "The Southern Cotton Association, 1905–1908." *J S Hist,* XIII (1947), 492-510.

16 SALOUTOS, Theodore and John D. HICKS. *Agricultural Discontent in the Middle West, 1900–1939.* Madison, Wis., 1951.†

17 SHANNON, Fred A. "The Status of the Midwestern Farmer in 1900." *Miss Val Hist Rev,* XXXVII (1950), 491-510.

18 SIMKINS, Francis B. *Pitchfork Ben Tillman, South Carolinian.* See 7.26.

19 WOODWARD, C. Vann. *Tom Watson, Agrarian Rebel.* See 8.16.

H. INTELLECTUAL PROGRESSIVISM

20 AARON, Daniel. *Men of Good Hope.* New York, 1951.†

21 COMMAGER, Henry S. *The American Mind.* New Haven, 1950.†

22 CURTI, Merle E. *The Growth of American Thought.* 3rd ed. New York, 1964.

1   DORFMAN, Joseph. *The Economic Mind in American Civilization.* 5 vols. New York, 1946–1959.

2   DORFMAN, Joseph. *Thorstein Veblen and His America.* New York, 1934.

3   FORCEY, Charles. *The Crossroads of Liberalism: Croly, Weyl, Lippmann, and the Progressive Era, 1900–1925.* New York, 1961.

4   FOX, Daniel M. *Discovery of Abundance: Simon N. Patten and the Transformation of Social Theory.* Ithaca, N.Y., 1967.

5   GABRIEL, Ralph H. *The Course of American Democratic Thought.* 2nd ed. New York, 1956.

6   GOLDMAN, Eric F. *Rendezvous with Destiny.* New York, 1953.†

7   HARTZ, Louis. *The Liberal Tradition in America.* New York, 1955.†

8   HOOK, Sidney. *John Dewey.* New York, 1939.

9   LASCH, Christopher. *The New Radicalism in America, 1889–1963.* New York, 1965.†

10   MANN, Arthur. "British Social Thought and American Reformers of the Progressive Era." *Miss Val Hist Rev,* XLII (1956), 672-692.

11   MASON, Alpheus T. *Brandeis. See 7.4.*

12   NOBLE, David W. "The New Republic and the Idea of Progress, 1914–1920." *Miss Val Hist Rev,* XXXVIII (1951), 387-402.

13   NOBLE, David W. *The Paradox of Progressive Thought.* Minneapolis, 1958.

14   VANCE, Maurice M. *Charles Van Hise. See 8.7.*

15   WHITE, Morton. *Social Thought in America.* New York, 1949.†

4. The Republican Era, 1901–1913

16   ADAMS, Graham, Jr. *Age of Industrial Violence, 1910–1915.* New York, 1966.

17   ANDERSON, Oscar E., Jr. *The Health of a Nation: Harvey W. Wiley and the Fight for Pure Food.* Chicago, 1958.

18   BLUM, John M. *The Republican Roosevelt.* Cambridge, Mass., 1954.†

19   BRAEMAN, John "The Square Deal in Action: A Case Study in the Growth of the 'National Police Power.' " *Change and Continuity in Twentieth-Century America.* Ed. by John Braeman, *et al.* Columbus, Ohio, 1964.

20   BUTT, Archibald W. *Taft and Roosevelt. See* 4.18.

21   CLAY, Howard B.. "Daniel Augustus Tompkins: The Role of the New South Industrialist in Politics." *East Carolina College Publications in History,* III (1966), 85-118.

22   CORNELL, Robert J. *The Anthracite Coal Strike of 1902.* Washington, D. C., 1957.

23   CROLY, Herbert D. *Marcus Alonzo Hanna.* See 5.1.

24   FOWLER, Dorothy. *John Coit Spooner.* See 5.8.

25   GARRATY, John A. *Right-Hand Man.* See 5.11.

26   GATEWOOD, Willard B. "Theodore Roosevelt and the Coinage Controversy." *Am Q,* XVIII (1966), 35-51.

1   GWINN, William Rea. *Uncle Joe Cannon, Archfoe of Insurgency.* See **5.23**.

2   HAGEDORN, Hermann. *The Roosevelt Family of Sagamore Hill.* See **5.25**.

3   HARBAUGH, William H. *Power and Responsibility.* See **6.1**.

4   HECHLER, Kenneth W. *Insurgency: Personalities and Politics of the Taft Era.* New York, 1940.

5   HOLLINGSWORTH, J. Rogers. *The Whirligig of Politics.* See **3.8**.

6   HOLT, James. *Congressional Insurgents and the Party System, 1909–1916.* Cambridge, Mass., 1967. (A study of the progressive faction within the Republican party.)

7   HORNIG, Edgar Albert. "The Religious Issue in the Taft-Bryan Duel of 1908." *Proc Am Philos Soc,* CV (1961), 530-537.

8   HOWE, M. A. De Wolfe. *George von Lengerke Meyer.* See **6.7**.

9   JESSUP, Philip C. *Elihu Root.* See **6.10**.

10   JOHNSON, Arthur M. "Antitrust Policy in Transition, 1908: Ideal and Reality." *Miss Val Hist Rev,* XLVIII (1961), 415-434.

11   JOHNSON, Carolyn W. *Winthrop Murray Crane: A Study in Republican Leadership, 1892–1920.* Northampton, Mass., 1967.

12   LA FOLLETTE, Belle C. and Fola. *Robert M. La Follette.* See **6.14**.

13   LAMBERT, Oscar D. *Stephen Benton Elkins.* See **6.16**.

14   LEOPOLD, Richard W. *Elihu Root and the Conservative Tradition.* See **6.19**.

15   LINK, Arthur S. "Theodore Roosevelt in His Letters." *Yale Rev,* XLIII (1954), 589-598.

16   LOWITT, Richard. "George Norris, James J. Hill, and the Railroad Rate Bill." *Neb Hist,* XL (1959), 137-146.

17   MASON, Alpheus T. *Bureaucracy Convicts Itself: The Ballinger-Pinchot Controversy of 1910.* New York, 1941.

18   MC GEARY, M. Nelson. *Gifford Pinchot, Forester-Politician.* See **7.7**.

19   MEYER, Balthasar Henry. *A History of the Northern Securities Case.* Madison, Wis., 1906.

20   MORISON, Elting E. *Turmoil and Tradition.* See **7.8**.

21   MORISON, Elting E. and John M. BLUM, eds. *The Letters of Theodore Roosevelt.* See **7.9**.

22   MOWRY, George E. *The Era of Theodore Roosevelt, 1900–1912.* New York, 1958.†

23   MOWRY, George E. *Theodore Roosevelt and the Progressive Movement.* Madison, Wis., 1946.†

24   O'GARA, Gordon C. *Theodore Roosevelt and the Rise of the Modern Navy.* Princeton, 1943.

25   PENICK, James, Jr. *Progressive Politics and Conservation.* See **15.7**.

26   PINKETT, Harold T. "The Keep Commission, 1905–1909: A Rooseveltian Effort for Administrative Reform." *J Am Hist,* LII (1965), 297-312.

27   PITKIN, William A. "Issues in the Roosevelt-Taft Contest of 1912." *Mid-Am,* XXXIV (1952), 219-232.

28   PRINGLE, Henry F. *The Life and Times of William Howard Taft.* See **7.17**.

1   PRINGLE, Henry F. *Theodore Roosevelt.* See **7.18.**

2   RIPLEY, William Z. *Railroads: Rates and Regulation.* New York, 1912.

3   ROOSEVELT, Theodore. *An Autobiography.* See **7.20.**

4   *The Works of Theodore Roosevelt.* See **7.21.**

5   SAGE, Leland L. *William Boyd Allison.* See **7.24.**

6   SCHEINBERG, Stephen J. "Theodore Roosevelt and the A. F. of L.'s Entry into Politics,1906–1908." *Lab Hist,* III (1962), 131-148.

7   SCHEINER, Seth M. "President Theodore Roosevelt and the Negro, 1901–1908." *J Neg Hist,* XLVII (1963), 169-183.

8   SOLVICK, Stanley D. "William Howard Taft and the Payne-Aldrich Tariff." *Miss Val Hist Rev,* L (1963), 424-442.

9   STEELMAN, Joseph F. "Republican Party Politics in North Carolina, 1902: Factions, Leaders, and Issues." *East Carolina College Publications in History,* III (1966), 119-150.

10 STEPHENSON, Nathaniel W. *Nelson W. Aldrich.* See **8.3.**

11 THORNBROUGH, Emma Lou. "The Brownsville Episode and the Negro Vote." *Miss Val Hist Rev,* XLIV (1957), 469-493.

12 TINSLEY, James A. "Roosevelt, Foraker, and the Brownsville Affray." *J Neg Hist,* XLI (1956), 43-65.

13 VAN RIPER, Paul P. *History of the United States Civil Service.* Evanston, Ill., 1958.

14 WARNER, Robert M. "Chase S. Osborn and the Presidential Campaign of 1912." *Miss Val Hist Rev,* XLVI (1959), 19-45.

15 WIEBE, Robert H. "The Anthracite Strike of 1902: A Record of Confusion." *Miss Val Hist Rev,* XLVIII (1961), 229-251.

16 WIEBE, Robert H. "The House of Morgan and the Executive, 1905–1913." *Am Hist Rev,* LXV (1959), 49-60.

17 WILENSKY, Norman M. *Conservatives in the Progressive Era: The Taft Republicans of 1912.* Gainsville, Fla., 1965.

5. The Wilson Era, 1913–1920

A. GENERAL

18 BABSON, Roger W. *W. B. Wilson and the Department of Labor.* New York, 1919.

19 BAKER, Ray Stannard. *Woodrow Wilson.* See **4.4.**

20 BAKER, Ray Stannard and William E. DODD, eds. *The Public Papers of Woodrow Wilson.* See **4.5.**

21 BELL, Herbert C. F. *Woodrow Wilson and the People.* See **4.8.**

22 BLUM, John M. *Joe Tumulty and the Wilson Era.* See **4.10.**

23 BLUM, John M. "Woodrow Wilson: A Study in Intellect." *Confluence,* V (1957), 367-376.

24 BLUM, John M. *Woodrow Wilson and the Politics of Morality.* See **4.11.**

1   BRAGDON, Henry W. *Woodrow Wilson.* See **4.14.**

2   BURNER, David. *The Politics of Provincialism: The Democratic Party in Transition, 1918–1932.* New York, 1968.

3   CRONON, E. David, ed. *The Cabinet Diaries of Josephus Daniels.* See **5.2.**

4   CRONON, E. David, ed. *The Political Thought of Woodrow Wilson.* Indianapolis, 1965.

5   DANIELS, Josephus. *The Wilson Era.* See **5.5.**

6   DAVIDSON, John Wells, ed. *A Crossroads of Freedom: The 1912 Campaign Speeches of Woodrow Wilson.* New Haven, 1956.

7   DE JOUVENEL, Bertrand. "Woodrow Wilson." *Confluence,* V (1957), 320-331.

8   DIAMOND, William. *The Economic Thought of Woodrow Wilson.* Baltimore, 1943.

9   DIMOCK, Marshall E. "Woodrow Wilson as Legislative Leader." *J Pol,* XIX (1957), 3-19.

10   FERRELL, Robert H. "Woodrow Wilson: Man and Statesman." *Rev Pol,* XVIII (1956), 131-145.

11   FREIDEL, Frank. *Franklin D. Roosevelt.* See **5.9.**

12   GARRATY, John A. *Henry Cabot Lodge.* See **5.10.**

13   GARRATY, John A. *Woodrow Wilson.* See **5.12.**

14   GARRATY, John A. "Woodrow Wilson: A Study in Personality." See **5.13.**

15   GEORGE, Alexander L. and Juliette L. *Woodrow Wilson and Colonel House.* See **5.15.**

16   GRAYSON, Cary T. *Woodrow Wilson.* See **5.22.**

17   GREENLEE, Howard Scott. "The Republican Party in Division and Reunion, 1913–1920." Doctoral dissertation, University of Chicago, 1950.

18   HECKSCHER, August. "Wilson–Style in Leadership." *Confluence,* V (1957), 332-340.

19   HECKSCHER, August, ed. *The Politics of Woodrow Wilson.* New York, 1956.

20   HOLT, James. *Congressional Insurgents and the Party System, 1909–1916.* See **17.6.**

21   HOUSTON, David F. *Eight Years with Wilson's Cabinet, 1913 to 1920.* See **6.5.**

22   HUTCHINSON, William T. *Lowden of Illinois.* See **6.8.**

23   KERNEY, James. *The Political Education of Woodrow Wilson.* See **6.13.**

24   LA FOLLETTE, Belle C. and Fola. *Robert M. La Follette.* See **6.14.**

25   LANE, Anne W. and Louise H. WALL, eds. *The Letters of Franklin K. Lane, Personal and Political.* See **6.17.**

26   LATHAM, Earl, ed. *The Philosophy and Politics of Woodrow Wilson.* Chicago, 1958.

27   LINK, Arthur S. "The Higher Realism of Woodrow Wilson." *J Presby Hist,* XLI (1963), 1-13.

28   LINK, Arthur S., *et al.,* eds. *The Papers of Woodrow Wilson.* See **6.21.**

1   LINK, Arthur S. *Wilson: The Road to the White House.* See **6.25**.

2   LINK, Arthur S. *Woodrow Wilson: A Brief Biography.* See **6.27**

3   LINK, Arthur S. *Woodrow Wilson and the Progressive Era.* New York, 1954.†

4   MC ADOO, William G. *Crowded Years.* See **7.6**.

5   NICHOLAS, Herbert G. "Wilsonianism at Mid-Century." *Centenaire Woodrow Wilson.* Geneva, 1956.

6   PAXSON, Frederic L. *American Democracy and the World War.* 3 vols. Boston, 1936–1948.

7   ROPER, Daniel C. *Fifty Years of Public Life.* See **7.22**.

8   SEYMOUR, Charles. *The Intimate Papers of Colonel House.* See **7.25**.

9   SEYMOUR, Charles. "Woodrow Wilson in Perspective." *For Aff,* XXXIV (1956), 175-186.

10   SMITH, John S. "Organized Labor and Government in the Wilson Era, 1913–1921: Some Conclusions." *Lab Hist,* III (1962), 265-286.

11   TINDALL, George Brown. *The Emergence of the New South.* See **3.23**.

12   VEYSEY, Laurence R. "The Academic Mind of Woodrow Wilson." *Miss Val Hist Rev,* XLIX (1963), 613-634.

13   WALWORTH, Arthur. *Woodrow Wilson.* See **8.11**.

14   WEINSTEIN, Edwin A. "Denial of Presidential Disability: A Case Study of Woodrow Wilson." *Psychiatry,* XXX (1967), 376-391.

B. THE NEW FREEDOM

15   ABRAMS, Richard M. "Woodrow Wilson and the Southern Congressmen, 1913–1916." *J S Hist,* XXII (1956), 417-437.

16   BATES, J. Leonard. *The Origins of Teapot Dome.* See **14.21**.

17   BLUMENTHAL, Henry. "Woodrow Wilson and the Race Question." *J Neg Hist,* XLVIII (1963), 1-21.

18   BURNER, David. "The Breakup of the Wilson Coalition of 1916." *Mid-Am,* XLV (1963), 18-35.

19   CLARK, John D. *The Federal Trust Policy.* See **2.12**.

20   DAVIDSON, John Wells. "The Response of the South to Woodrow Wilson's New Freedom, 1912–1914." Doctoral dissertation, Yale University, 1954.

21   DAVIS, G. Cullom. "The Transformation of the Federal Trade Commission, 1914–1929." *Miss Val Hist Rev,* XLIX (1962), 437-455.

22   GLASS, Carter. *An Adventure in Constructive Finance.* Garden City, N.Y., 1927.

23   GRANTHAM, Dewey W., Jr. "Southern Congressional Leaders and the New Freedom, 1913–1917." *J S Hist,* XIII (1947), 439-459.

24   HARRIS, Seymour E. *Twenty Years of the Federal Reserve Policy.* 2 vols. Cambridge, Mass., 1933.

25   HOHMAN, Elmo Paul. "Maritime Labour in the United States: The Seamen's Act and Its Historical Background." *Int Lab Rev,* XXXVIII (1938), 190-218.

1   ISE, John. *The United States Oil Policy*. New Haven, 1926.

2   KEMMERER, Edwin W. "Six Years of Postal Savings in the United States." *Am Econ Rev*, VII (1917), 46-90.

3   KERR, James J., IV. "German-Americans and Neutrality in the 1916 Election." *Mid-Am*, XLIII (1961), 95-105.

4   KLEBANER, Benjamin J. "Potential Competition and the American Antitrust Legislation of 1914." *Bus Hist Rev*, XXXVIII (1964), 163-185.

5   LAUGHLIN, J. Laurence. *The Federal Reserve Act: Its Origins and Problems*. New York, 1933.

6   LEARY, William M., Jr. "Woodrow Wilson, Irish Americans, and the Election of 1916." *J Am Hist*, LIV (1967), 57-72.

7   LINK, Arthur S. "The Baltimore Convention of 1912." *Am Hist Rev*, L (1945), 691-713.

8   LINK, Arthur S. "The Negro as a Factor in the Campaign of 1912." *J Neg Hist*, XXXII (1947), 81-99.

9   LINK, Arthur S. "The South and the Democratic Campaign of 1910–1912." Doctoral dissertation, University of North Carolina, 1945.

10 LINK, Arthur S. "The South and the 'New Fredom': An Interpretation." *Am Sch*, XX (1951), 314-324.

11 LINK, Arthur S. "The Underwood Presidential Movement of 1912." *J S Hist*, XI (1945), 230-245.

12 LINK, Arthur S. *Wilson: Campaigns for Progressivism and Peace,1916–1917*. See **6.22**.

13 LINK,   Arthur S. *Wilson: The New Freedom*. See **6.24**.

14 MC GOVERN, George S. "The Colorado Coal Strike,1913–1914." Doctoral dissertation, Northwestern University, 1953.

15 MURRAY, Robert K. "Public Opinion, Labor, and the Clayton Act." *Historian*, XXI (1959), 255-270.

16 PERKINS, Dexter. *Charles Evans Hughes and American Democratic Statesmanship*. See **7.16**.

17 PORTER, Eugene. "The Colorado Coal Strike of 1913: An Interpretation." *Historian*, XII (1949), 3-27.

18 PUSEY, Merlo J. *Charles Evans Hughes*. See **7.19**.

19 RATNER, Sidney. *American Taxation*. See **3.17**.

20 RUBLEE, George. "The Original Plan and Early History of the Federal Trade Commission." *Proc Acad Pol Sci*, XI (1926), 114-120.

21 SEAGER, Henry R. and Charles A. GULICK. *Trust and Corporation Problems*. See **3.18**.

22 SHARFMAN, I. L. *The Interstate Commerce Commission*. See **3.19**.

23 SMITH, Rixey and Norman BEASLEY. *Carter Glass*. See **7.27**.

24 TAUSSIG, Frank W. *Tariff History of the United State*. See **3.21**.

25 TODD, A. L. *Justice on Trial: The Case of Louis D. Brandeis*. New York, 1964.

26 UROFSKY, Melvin I. "Wilson, Brandeis and the Trust Issue, 1912–1914." *Mid-Am*, XLIX (1967), 3-28.

1 WARBURG, Paul M. *Essays on Banking Reform in the United States.* New York, 1914.

2 WARBURG, Paul M. *The Federal Reserve System.* 2 vols. New York, 1930.

3 WILLIS, Henry Parker. *The Federal Reserve System.* New York, 1923.

4 WOLGEMUTH, Kathleen Long. "Woodrow Wilson's Appointment Policy and the Negro." *J S Hist,* XXIV (1958), 457-471.

C. THE FIRST WORLD WAR AND AFTER

5 ABRAMS, Ray H. *Preachers Present Arms: A Study of Wartime Attitudes and Activities of the Churches and the Clergy in the United States, 1914–1918.* Philadelphia, 1933.

6 ADLER, Selig. "The Congressional Election of 1918." *S Atl Q,* XXXVI (1937), 447-465.

7 ARNETT, Alex Mathews. *Claude Kitchin and the Wilson War Policies.* Boston, 1937.

8 BAGBY, Wesley M. *The Road to Normalcy: The Presidential Campaign and Election of 1920.* Baltimore, 1962.

9 BARUCH, Bernard M. *American Industry in the War.* New York, 1941.

10 BEAVER, Daniel R. *Newton D. Baker and the American War Effort, 1917–1919.* Lincoln, Neb., 1966.

11 BEAVER, Daniel R. "Newton D. Baker and the Genesis of the War Industries Board, 1917–1918." *J Am Hist,* LII (1965), 43-58.

12 BING, Alexander M. *War-time Strikes and Their Adjustment.* New York, 1921.

13 BLUM, John M. "Nativism, Anti-Radicalism, and the Foreign Scare, 1917–1920." *Midwest Journal,* III (1950–1951), 46-53.

14 BOGART, Ernest Ludlow. *War Costs and Their Financing.* New York, 1921.

15 BRODY, David. *Labor in Crisis: The Steel Strike of 1919.* Philadelphia, 1965.†

16 BURNER, David. *The Politics of Provincialism.* See **19.2.**

17 CHAFEE, Zechariah, Jr. *Free Speech in the United States.* Cambridge, Mass., 1941.

18 Chicago Commission on Race Relations. *The Negro in Chicago: A Study of Race Relations and a Race Riot.* Chicago, 1922.

19 CLARK, John Maurice. *The Costs of the World War to the American People.* New Haven, 1931.

20 CLARKSON, Grosvenor B. *Industrial America in the World War.* Boston, 1923.

21 COBEN, Stanley. *A. Mitchell Palmer.* See **4.19.**

22 COBEN, Stanley. "A Study in Nativism: The American Red Scare of 1919–1920." *Pol Sci Q,* LXXIX (1964), 52-75.

23 COIT, Margaret L. *Mr. Baruch.* See **4.20.**

24 COSTRELL, Edwin. *How Maine Viewed the War, 1914–1917.* Orono, Me., 1940.

25 CRAMER, Clarence H. *Newton D. Baker.* See **4.23.**

1   CRIGHTON, John C. *Missouri and the World War, 1914–1917.* Columbia, Mo., 1947.

2   CROWELL, Benedict and Robert Frost WILSON. *How America Went to War.* 6 vols. New Haven, 1921.

3   CUFF, Robert D. "A 'Dollar-a-Year Man' in Government: George N. Peek and the War Industries Board." *Bus Hist Rev,* XLI (1967), 404-420.

4   CUMMINS, Cedric C. *Indiana Public Opinion and the World War,1914–1917.* Indianapolis, 1945.

5   CURTI, Merle E. *The Roots of American Loyalty.* New York, 1946.

6   DAVIS, Allen F. "Welfare, Reform and World War I." *Am Q,* XIX (1967), 516-533.

7   DRAPER, Theodore. *The Roots of American Communism.* New York, 1957.†

8   GOLDMAN, Eric F. "Woodrow Wilson: The Test of War." *Woodrow Wilson and the World of Today.* Ed. by Arthur P. Dudden. Philadelphia, 1957.

9   HAGEDORN, Hermann. *Leonard Wood.* See **5.24**.

10 HIMMELBERG, Robert F. "The War Industries Board and the Antitrust Question in November 1918." *J Am Hist,* LII (1965), 59-74.

11 HINES, Walker D. *War History of American Railroads.* New Haven, 1928.

12 HOVENSTINE, E. Jay, Jr. "Lessons of World War I." *Ann Am Acad Pol Soc Sci,* CCXXXVIII (1945), 180-187.

13 HURLEY, Edward N. *The Bridge to France.* Philadelphia, 1927.

14 Interchurch World Movement of North America. *Report on the Steel Strike of 1919.* New York, 1920.

15 JOHNSON, Donald D. *The Challenge to American Freedoms: World War I and the Rise of the American Civil Liberties Union.* Lexington, Ky., 1963.

16 KAPLAN, Sidney. "Social Engineers as Saviors: Effects of World War I on Some American Liberals." *J Hist Ideas,* XVII (1956), 347-369.

17 KERR, K. Austin. "Decision for Federal Control: Wilson, McAdoo, and the Railroads, 1917." *J Am Hist,* LIV (1967), 550-560.

18 KESTER, Randall B. "The War Industries Board, 1917–1918: A Study in Industrial Mobilization." *Am Pol Sci Rev,* XXXIV (1940), 655-684.

19 KOISTINEN, Paul A. C. "The 'Industrial-Military Complex' in Historical Perspective: World War I." *Bus Hist Rev,* XLI (1967), 378-403.

20 LASSWELL, Harold D. *Propaganda Technique in the World War.* New York, 1927.

21 LEUCHTENBURG, William E. "The New Deal and the Analogue of War." *Change and Continuity in Twentieth-Century America.* Ed. by John Braeman, et al. Columbus, Ohio, 1964.

22 LEVINE, Lawrence W. *Defender of the Faith.* See **6.20**.

23 LIVERMORE, Seward W. *Politics Is Adjourned: Woodrow Wilson and the War Congress, 1916–1918.* Middletown, Conn., 1966.

24 LIVERMORE, Seward W. "The Section Issue in the 1918 Congressional Elections." *Miss Val Hist Rev,* XXXV (1948), 29-60.

25 MOCK, James R. and Cedric LARSON. *Words that Won the War: The Story of the Committee on Public Information, 1917–1919.* Princeton, 1939.

26 MOCK, James R. and Evangeline THURBER. *Report on Demobilization.* Norman, Okla., 1944.

1 MULLENDORE, William C. *History of the United States Food Administration, 1917–1919.* Stanford, 1941.

2 MURRAY, Robert K. "Communism and the Great Steel Strike of 1919." *Miss Val Hist Rev,* XXXVIII (1951), 445-466.

3 MURRAY, Robert K. *Red Scare: A Study in National Hysteria, 1919–1920.* Minneapolis, 1955.†

4 NASH, Gerald D. "Franklin D. Roosevelt and Labor: The World War I Origins of the Early New Deal Policy." *Lab Hist,* I (1960), 39-52.

5 NEWBY, I. A. "States' Rights and Southern Congressmen during World War I." *Phylon,* XXIV (1963), 34-50.

6 NOYES, Alexander D. *The War Period of American Finance, 1908–1925.* New York, 1926.

7 PALMER, Frederick. *Newton D. Baker.* See **7.15**.

8 PAXSON, Frederic L. *American Democracy and the World War.* See **20.6**.

9 PAXSON, Frederic L. "The American War Government, 1917–1918." *Am Hist Rev,* XXVI (1920), 54-76.

10 PAXSON, Frederic L. "The Great Demobilization." *Am Hist Rev,* XLIV (1939), 237-251.

11 PETERSON, Horace C. *Propaganda for War.* Norman, Okla., 1939.

12 PETERSON, Horace C. and Gilbert C. FITE. *Opponents of War, 1917–1918.* Madison, Wis., 1957.

13 PRESTON, William, Jr. *Aliens and Dissenters: Federal Suppression of Radicals, 1903–1933.* Cambridge, Mass., 1963.†

14 RUDWICK, Elliot M. *Race Riot at East St. Louis, July 2, 1917.* Carbondale, Ill., 1964.†

15 SCHEIBER, Harry N. *The Wilson Administration and Civil Liberties, 1917–1921.* Ithaca, N.Y., 1960.

16 SLOSSON, Preston W. *The Great Crusade and After, 1914–1928.* New York, 1940.

17 SMITH, Daniel M. "Lansing and the Wilson Interregnum, 1919–1920." *Historian,* XXI (1959), 135-161.

18 SWISHER, Carl Brent. "Civil Liberties in War Time." *Pol Sci Q,* LV (1940), 321-347.

19 SWISHER, Carl Brent. "The Control of War Preparations in the United States." *Am Pol Sci Rev,* XXXIV (1940), 1085-1103.

20 TAFT, Philip. "The Federal Trials of the I.W.W." *Lab Hist,* III (1962), 57-91.

21 TOBIN, Harold J. and Percy W. BIDWELL. *Mobilizing Civilian America.* New York, 1940.

22 TRATTNER, Walter I. "Progressivism and World War I: A Re-appraisal." *Mid-Am,* XLIV (1962), 131-145.

23 TURLINGTON, Edgar W. "The World War Period." *Neutrality, Its History, Economics and Law.* Ed. by Philip C. Jessup, *et al.* New York, 1936.

24 VIERECK, George Sylvester. *Spreading Germs of Hate.* New York, 1930.

1   WARD, Robert D. "The Origins and Activities of the National Security League, 1914–1919." *Miss Val Hist Rev*, XLVII (1960), 51-65.

2   WARTH, Robert D. "The Palmer Raids." *S Atl Q*, XLVIII (1949), 1-23.

3   WATKINS, Gordon S. *Labor Problems and the Labor Administration in the United States during the World War*. Urbana, Ill., 1920.

4   WEINBERG, Sydney. "What to Tell America: The Writers' Quarrel in the Office of War Information." *J Am Hist*, LV (1968), 73-89.

5   WEINSTEIN, Edwin A. "Denial of Presidential Disability: A Case Study of Woodrow Wilson." See **20.14**.

6   WEINSTEIN, James. "Anti-War Sentiment and the Socialist Party, 1917–1918." *Pol Sci Q*, LXXIV (1959), 215-239.

7   WILLIAMS, Michael. *American Catholics in the War: National Catholic War Council, 1917–1921*. New York, 1921.

8   WILLOUGHBY, William Franklin. *Government Organization in War Time and After*. New York, 1919.

9   WITTKE, Carl. *German-Americans and the World War*. Columbus, Ohio, 1936.

10   WRESZIN, Michael. *Oswald Garrison Villard: Pacifist at War*. Bloomington, Ind., 1965.

6. The Supreme Court

11   BOUDIN, Louis B. *Government by Judiciary*. 2 vols. New York, 1932.

12   CORWIN, Edward S. *Commerce Power versus States' Rights*. Princeton, 1936.

13   CORWIN, Edward S. *Court over Constitution*. Princeton, 1938.

14   CORWIN, Edward S. *The Twilight of the Supreme Court*. New Haven, 1934.

15   DUNNE, Gerald T. *Monetary Decisions of the Supreme Court*. New Brunswick, N.J., 1960.

16   FINKELSTEIN, Maurice. "From *Munn v. Illinois* to *Tyson v. Banton*: A Study in the Judicial Process." *Columbia Law Review*, XXVII (1927), 769-783.

17   FRANKFURTER, Felix. *Mr. Justice Holmes and the Supreme Court*. Cambridge, Mass., 1938.†

18   GARRATY, John A. "Holmes's Appointment to the U.S. Supreme Court." *N Eng Q*, XXII (1949), 291-303.

19   GOEDECKE, Robert. "Holmes, Brandeis, and Frankfurter: Differences in Pragmatic Jurisprudence." *Ethics*, LXXIV (1964), 83-96.

20   HAMILTON, Walton H. "The Path of Due Process of Law." *The Constitution Reconsidered*. Ed. by Conyers Read. New York, 1938.

21   KELLER, Morton. "The Judicial System and the Law of Life Insurance, 1888–1910." *Bus Hist Rev*, XXXV (1961), 317-335.

22   KELLY, Alfred H. and Winfred A. HARBISON. *The American Constitution*. 3rd ed. New York, 1963.

23   KING, Willard L. *Melville Weston Fuller: Chief Justice of the United States, 1888–1910*. New York, 1950.†

24   KLINKHAMER, Marie Carolyn. *Edward Douglas White, Chief Justice of the United States*. Washington, D.C., 1943.

1 KUTLER, Stanley I. "Labor, the Clayton Act, and the Supreme Court." *Lab Hist,* III (1962), 19-38.

2 LERNER, Max. *The Mind and Faith of Justice Holmes.* Boston, 1943.

3 MASON, Alpheus T. *Brandeis.* See **7.4.**

4 MOTT, Rodney L. *Due Process of Law.* Indianapolis, 1926.

5 PERKINS, Dexter. *Charles Evans Hughes and American Democratic Statesmanship.* See **7.16.**

6 PUSEY, Merlo J. *Charles Evans Hughes.* See **7.19.**

7 ROCHE, John P. "Entrepreneurial Liberty and the Fourteenth Amendment." *Lab Hist,* IV (1963), 3-31.

8 ROELOFS, Vernon, W. "Justice William R. Day and Federal Regulation." *Miss Val Hist Rev,* XXXVII (1950), 39-60.

9 RUMBLE, Wilfrid E., Jr. "Legal Realism, Sociological Jurisprudence and Mr. Justice Holmes." *J Hist Ideas,* XXVI (1965), 547-566.

10 TODD, A. L. *Justice on Trial.* See **21.25.**

11 TWISS, Benjamin R. *Lawyers and the Constitution.* Princeton, 1942.

12 WARREN, Charles. *The Supreme Court in United States History.* 2 vols. Boston, 1926.

13 WOOD, Stephen B. *Constitutional Politics in the Progressive Era.* See **13.21.**

7. Socialism

14 BEDFORD, Henry F. *Socialism and the Workers in Massachusetts, 1886–1912.* Amherst, Mass., 1966.

15 BRISSENDEN, Paul F. *The I.W.W.* New York, 1919.

16 EGBERT, Donald D. and Stow PERSONS, eds. *Socialism and American Life.* 2 vols. Princeton, 1952.

17 GINGER, Ray. *The Bending Cross.* See **5.16.**

18 HANDY, Robert T. "Christianity and Socialism in America, 1900–1920." *Church Hist,* XXI (1952), 39-54.

19 HILLQUIT, Morris. *History of Socialism in the United States.* New York, 1910.

20 KIPNIS, Ira A. *The American Socialist Movement, 1897–1912.* New York, 1952.

21 MORGAN, H. Wayne. *Eugene V. Debs: Socialist for President.* Syracuse, 1962.

22 MORGAN, H. Wayne. "Eugene Debs and the Socialist Campaign of 1912." *Mid-Am,* XXXIX (1957), 210-226.

23 QUINT, Howard H. *The Forging of American Socialism.* Columbia, S.C., 1953.†

24 SHANNON, David A. "The Socialist Party Before the First World War: An Analysis." *Miss Val Hist Rev,* XXXVIII (1951), 279-288.

25 SHANNON, David A. *The Socialist Party of America: A History.* New York, 1955.†

26 WEINSTEIN, James. "Anti-War Sentiment and the Socialist Party, 1917–1918." See **25.6.**

27 WEINSTEIN, James. *The Decline of Socialism in America, 1912–1925.* New York, 1967.

III. The United States and Its World Relations

1. General

1   ADLER, Selig. *The Isolationist Impulse.* New York, 1957.†

2   BAILEY, Thomas A. "America's Emergence as a World Power: The Myth and the Verity." *Pac Hist Rev,* XXX (1961), 1-16.

3   BAILEY, Thomas A. *The Man in the Street: The Impact of American Public Opinion on Foreign Policy.* New York, 1948.

4   BAILEY, Thomas A. "The World Cruise of the American Battleship Fleet, 1907–1909." *Pac Hist Rev,* I (1932), 389-423.

5   BEALE, Howard K. *Theodore Roosevelt and the Rise of America to World Power.* Baltimore, 1956.†

6   BEMIS, Samuel Flagg. *A Diplomatic History of the United States.* 5th ed. New York, 1965.

7   BLAKE, Nelson Manfred. "Ambassadors at the Court of Theodore Roosevelt." *Miss Val Hist Rev,* XLII (1955), 179-206.

8   BULLOCK, Charles T., *et al.* "The Balance of Trade of the United States." *Rev Econ Stat,* I (1919), 245-246.

9   COLETTA, Paolo E. "Secretary of State William Jennings Bryan and 'Deserving Democrats.'" *Mid-Am,* XLVIII (1966), 75-98.

10   DAVIS, George T. *A Navy Second to None.* New York, 1940.

11   DULLES, Foster Rhea. *America's Rise to World Power, 1898–1954.* New York, 1955.†

12   DUROSELLE, Jean Baptiste. *From Wilson to Roosevelt: Foreign Policy of the United States, 1913–1945.* Cambridge, Mass., 1963.†

13   ELLIS, L. Ethan. *Reciprocity, 1911.* New Haven, 1939.

14   ERSHKOWITZ, Herbert. *The Attitude of Business Toward American Foreign Policy, 1900–1916.* University Park, Pa., 1967.

15   FILENE, Peter. "The World Peace Foundation and Progressivism, 1910–1918." *N Eng Q,* XXXVI (1963), 478-501.

16   GRAEBNER, Norman A., ed. *An Uncertain Tradition: American Secretaries of State in the Twentieth Century.* New York, 1961.†

17   GREENE, Fred. "The Military View of American National Policy, 1904–1940." *Am Hist Rev,* LXVI (1961), 354-377.

18   GRENVILLE, John A. S. and George Berkeley YOUNG. *Politics, Strategy, and American Diplomacy: Studies in Foreign Policy, 1873–1917.* New Haven, 1966.

19   HART, Robert A. *The Great White Fleet: Its Voyage Around the World, 1907–1909.* Boston, 1965.

20   KENNAN, George F. *American Diplomacy, 1900–1950.* Chicago, 1951.†

21   LEOPOLD, Richard W. "The Emergence of America as a World Power: Some Second Thoughts." *Change and Continuity in Twentieth-Century America.* Ed. by John Braeman, *et al.* Columbus, Ohio, 1964.

1   LEOPOLD, Richard W. *The Growth of American Foreign Policy.* New York, 1962.

2   LEOPOLD, Richard W. "The Mississippi Valley and American Foreign Policy, 1890–1941: An Assessment and an Appeal." *Miss Val Hist Rev,* XXXVII (1951), 625-642.

3   LEWIS, Cleona. *America's Stake in International Investments.* Washington, D.C., 1938.

4   LIVEZEY, William E. *Mahan on Sea Power.* Norman, Okla., 1947.

5   OSGOOD, Robert E. *Ideals and Self-Interest in America's Foreign Relations.* Chicago, 1953.†

6   PATTERSON, Thomas G. "American Businessmen and Consular Service Reform, 1890's to 1906." *Bus Hist Rev,* XL (1966), 77-97.

7   PRATT, Julius W. *Challenge and Rejection: The United States and World Leadership, 1900–1921.* New York, 1967.

8   SPROUT, Harold and Margaret. *The Rise of American Naval Power.* Princeton, 1939.†

9   STUART, Graham H. *The Department of State: A History of Its Organization, Procedure, and Personnel.* New York, 1949.

10 WILLIAMS, Benjamin H. *Economic Foreign Policy of the United States.* New York, 1929.

11 WILLIAMS, William A. *The Tragedy of American Diplomacy.* Cleveland, 1959.†

2. Imperialism and the War with Spain

12 AUXIER, George W. "Middle Western Newspapers and the Spanish-American War, 1895–1898." *Miss Val Hist Rev,* XXVI (1940), 523-534.

13 BAILEY, Thomas A. "Dewey and the Germans at Manila Bay." *Am Hist Rev,* XLV (1939), 58-81.

14 BURTON, David H. "Theodore Roosevelt: Confident Imperialist." *Rev Pol,* XXIII (1961), 365-377.

15 BURTON, David H. "Theodore Roosevelt's Social Darwinism and Views on Imperialism." *J Hist Ideas,* XXVI (1965), 103-118.

16 COLETTA, Paolo E. "Bryan, McKinley, and the Treaty of Paris." *Pac Hist Rev,* XXVI (1957), 131-146.

17 COLETTA, Paolo E. "McKinley, the Peace Negotiations, and the Acquisition of the Philippines." *Pac Hist Rev,* XXX (1961), 341-350.

18 DENNETT, Tyler. *John Hay.* New York, 1933.

19 DENNIS, A. L. P. "John Hay." *The American Secretaries of State and Their Diplomacy.* Ed. by Samuel Flagg Bemis. Vol. IX. New York, 1929.

20 DULLES, Foster Rhea. *The Imperial Years.* New York, 1956.

21 EYRE, James E., Jr. "Russia and the American Acquisition of the Philippines." *Miss Val Hist Rev,* XXVIII (1942), 539-562.

22 FARRELL, John T. "Archbishop Ireland and Manifest Destiny." *Cath Hist Rev,* XXXIII (1947), 269-301.

1   HARBAUGH, William H. *Power and Responsibility.* See **6.1**

2   HARRINGTON, Fred H. "The Anti-Imperialist Movement in the United States, 1898–1900." *Miss Val Hist Rev,* XXII (1935), 211,230.

3   HARRINGTON, Fred H. "Literary Aspects of American Anti-Imperialism, 1898–1902." *N Eng Q,* X (1937), 650-667.

4   HOFSTADTER, Richard. "Manifest Destiny and the Philippines." *America in Crisis.* Ed. by Daniel Aaron. New York, 1952.

5   KARRAKER, William Archibald. "The American Churches and the Spanish-American War." Doctoral dissertation, University of Chicago, 1940.

6   LASCH, Christopher. "The Anti-Imperialists, the Philippines, and the Inequality of Man." *J S Hist,* XXIV (1958), 319-331.

7   LEUCHTENBURG, William E. "Progressivism and Imperialism: The Progressive Movement and American Foreign Policy, 1898–1916." *Miss Val Hist Rev,* XXXIX (1952), 483-504.

8   MAY, Ernest R. "American Imperialism: A Reinterpretation." *Perspectives in American History,* I (1967), 123-286.

9   MAY, Ernest R. *Imperial Democracy.* New York, 1961.

10   MC CORMICK, Thomas. "Insular Imperialism and the Open Door: The China Market and the Spanish-American War." *Pac Hist Rev,* XXXII (1963), 155-170.

11   MC KEE, Delber L. "Samuel Gompers, the A. F. of L., and Imperialism, 1895–1900." *Historian,* XXI (1959), 187-199.

12   MORGAN, H. Wayne. *America's Road to Empire: The War with Spain and Overseas Expansion.* New York, 1965.

13   MORGAN, H. Wayne, ed. *Making Peace with Spain: The Diary of Whitelaw Reid.* Austin, Tex., 1965.

14   MORGAN, H. Wayne. *William McKinley and His America.* Syracuse, 1963.

15   MORISON, Elting E. and John M. BLUM, eds. *The Letters of Theodore Roosevelt.* See **7.9**.

16   NEALE, R. G. *Great Britain and United States Expansion: 1898–1900.* East Lansing, Mich., 1966.

17   OLCOTT, Charles S. *The Life of William McKinley.* 2 vols. Boston, 1916.

18   PRATT, Julius W. *America's Colonial Experiment.* New York, 1950.

19   PRATT, Julius W. *Expansionists of 1898.* Baltimore, 1936.

20   PRATT, Julius W. "The 'Large Policy' of 1898." *Miss Val Hist Rev,* XIX (1932), 219-242.

21   PULESTON, William D. *Mahan: The Life and Work of Captain Alfred Thayer Mahan, U.S.N.* New Haven, 1939.

22   QUINT, Howard H. "American Socialists and the Spanish-American War." *Am Q,* X (1958), 131-141.

23   REUTER, Frank T. *Catholic Influence on American Colonial Policies, 1898–1904.* Austin, Tex., 1967.

24   SEARS, Louis Martin. "John Sherman." *The American Secretaries of State and Their Diplomacy.* Ed. by Samuel Flagg Bemis. Vol. IX. New York, 1929.

1   SHIPPEE, Lester B. "Germany and the Spanish-American War." *Am Hist Rev*, XXX (1925), 754-777.

2   SHIPPEE, Lester B. and Royal B. WAY. "William Rufus Day." *The American Secretaries of State and Their Diplomacy.* Ed. by Samuel Flagg Bemis. Vol. IX. New York, 1929.

3   SWANBERG, W. A. *Citizen Hearst.* See 8.5.

4   SWANBERG, W. A. *Pulitzer.* See 8.6.

5   TOMPKINS, E. Berkeley. "Scylla and Charybdis: The Anti-Imperialist Dilemma in the Election of 1900." *Pac Hist Rev*, XXXVI (1967), 143-162.

6   WEINBERG, Albert K. *Manifest Destiny.* Baltimore, 1935.

7   WILKERSON, Marcus M. *Public Opinion and the Spanish-American War.* Baton Rouge, 1932.

8   WILLIAMS, William A. "Brooks Adams and American Expansion." *N Eng Q*, XXV (1952), 217-232.

9   WISAN, Joseph E. *The Cuban Crises as Reflected in the New York Press, 1895–1898.* New York, 1934.

3. The United States and Latin America

10   ADLER, Selig. "Bryan and Wilsonian Caribbean Penetration." *His-Am Hist Rev*, XX (1940), 198-226.

11   AMERINGER, Charles D. "The Panama Canal Lobby of Philippe Bunau-Varilla and William Nelson Cromwell." *Am Hist Rev*, LXVIII (1963), 346-363.

12   AMERINGER, Charles D. "Philippe Bunau-Varilla: New Light on the Panama Canal Treaty." *His-Am Hist Rev*, XLVI (1966), 28-52.

13   BAKER, George. "The Wilson Administration and Cuba, 1913–1921." *Mid-Am*, XLVI (1964), 48-74.

14   BEALE, Howard K. *Theodore Roosevelt and the Rise of America to World Power.* See 27.5.

15   BEMIS, Samuel Flagg. *The Latin American Policy of the United States.* New York, 1943.

16   BERBUSSE, Edward J. *The United States in Puerto Rico, 1898–1900.* Chapel Hill, 1966.

17   CALLCOTT, Wilfrid A. *The Caribbean Policy of the United States, 1890–1920.* Baltimore, 1942.

18   CALVERT, Peter. *The Mexican Revolution 1910–1914: The Diplomacy of Anglo-American Conflict.* Cambridge, Eng., 1968.

19   CLENDENEN, Clarence C. *The United States and Pancho Villa.* Ithaca, N.Y., 1961.

20   CLINE, Howard F. *The United States and Mexico.* Rev. ed. Cambridge, Mass., 1963.†

21   COLETTA, Paolo E. "William Jennings Bryan and the United States-Colombia Impasse, 1903–1921." *His-Am Hist Rev*, XLVII (1967), 486-501.

22   CUMBERLAND, Charles C. *The Mexican Revolution: Genesis Under Madero.* Austin, Tex., 1952.

23   DENNIS, A. L. P. *Adventures In American Diplomacy, 1896–1906.* New York, 1928.

1 FABELA, Isidro. *Historia Diplomática de la Revolución Mexicana.* 2 vols. Mexico City, 1958–1959.

2 FITZGIBBON, Russell H. *Cuba and the United States, 1900–1935.* Menasha, Wis., 1935.

3 [FULLER, Joseph V.] "William Jennings Bryan." *The American Secretaries of State and Their Diplomacy.* Ed. by Samuel Flagg Bemis. Vol. X. New York, 1929.

4 HAGEDORN, Hermann. *Leonard Wood.* See **5.24**.

5 HARBAUGH, William H. *Power and Responsibility.* See **6.1**.

6 HEALY, David F. *The United States in Cuba, 1898–1902.* Madison, Wis., 1963.

7 JESSUP, Philip. *Elihu Root.* See **6.10**.

8 KAHLE, Louis G. "Robert Lansing and the Recognition of Venustiana Carranza." *His-Am Hist Rev,* XXXVIII (1958), 353-372.

9 LEOPOLD, Richard W. *Elihu Root and the Conservative Tradition.* See **6.19**.

10 LINK, Arthur S. *Wilson: Campaigns for Progressivism and Peace, 1916–1917.* See **6.22**.

11 LINK, Arthur S. *Wilson: Confusions and Crises, 1915–1916.* See **6.23**.

12 LINK, Arthur S. *Wilson: The New Freedom.* See **6.24**.

13 LINK, Arthur S. *Wilson: The Struggle for Neutrality, 1914–1915.* See **6.26**.

14 LINK, Arthur S. *Woodrow Wilson and the Progressive Era.* See **20.3**.

15 LIVERMORE, Seward W. "Battleship Diplomacy in South America: 1905–1925." *J Mod Hist,* XVI (1944), 31-48.

16 LIVERMORE, Seward W. "Theodore Roosevelt, the American Navy, and the Venezuelan Crisis of 1902–1903." *Am Hist Rev,* LI (1946), 452-471.

17 LOCKMILLER, David A. *Magoon in Cuba: A History of the Second Intervention, 1906–1909.* Chapel Hill, 1938.

18 MC GANN, Thomas F. *Argentina, the United States, and the Inter-American System, 1880–1914.* Cambridge, Mass., 1957.

19 MINER, Dwight C. *The Fight for the Panama Route.* New York, 1940.

20 MINGER, Ralph Eldin. "William H. Taft and the United States Intervention in Cuba in 1906." *His-Am Hist Rev,* XLI (1961), 75-89.

21 MORISON, Elting E. and John M. BLUM, eds. *The Letters of Theodore Roosevelt.* See **7.9**.

22 MUNRO, Dana G. "Dollar Diplomacy in Nicaragua, 1909–1913." *His-Am Hist Rev,* XXXVIII (1958), 209-234.

23 MUNRO, Dana G. *The Five Republics of Central America.* New York, 1918.

24 MUNRO, Dana G. *Intervention and Dollar Diplomacy in the Caribbean, 1900–1921.* Princeton, 1964.

25 PERKINS, Dexter. *A History of the Monroe Doctrine.* Rev. ed. Boston, 1955.

26 PIKE, Frederick B. *Chile and the United States, 1880–1962.* Notre Dame, Ind., 1963.

1 PRATT, Julius W. "Robert Lansing." *The American Secretaries of State and Their Diplomacy*. Ed. by Samuel Flagg Bemis. Vol. X. New York, 1929.

2 PRINGLE, Henry F. *The Life and Times of William Howard Taft*. See **7.17**.

3 PRINGLE, Henry F. *Theodore Roosevelt*. See **7.18**.

4 QUIRK, Robert E. *An Affair of Honor: Woodrow Wilson and the Occupation of Veracruz*. Lexington, Ky., 1962.

5 QUIRK, Robert E. *The Mexican Revolution, 1914–1915: The Convention of Aguascalientes*. Bloomington, Ind., 1960.

6 RIPPY, J. Fred. "Antecedents of the Roosevelt Corollary of the Monroe Doctrine." *Pac Hist Rev*, IX (1940), 267-279.

7 RIPPY, J. Fred. *The Capitalists and Columbia*. New York, 1931.

8 ROOSEVELT, Theodore. *An Autobiography*. See **7.20**.

9 SCOTT, James B. "Elihu Root." *The American Secretaries of State and Their Diplomacy*. Ed. by Samuel Flagg Bemis. Vol. IX. New York, 1929.

10 STEPHENSON, George M. *John Lind of Minnesota*. Minneapolis, 1935.

11 TANSILL, Charles C. *The Purchase of the Danish West Indies*. Baltimore, 1932.

12 TURLINGTON, Edgar. *Mexico and Her Foreign Creditors*. New York, 1930.

13 WELLES, Sumner. *Naboth's Vineyard: The Dominican Republic, 1844–1924*. New York, 1928.

14 WRIGHT, Herbert F. "Philander C. Knox." *The American Secretaries of State and Their Diplomacy*. Ed. by Samuel Flagg Bemis. Vol. IX. New York, 1929.

4. The United States and Europe

15 ALLEN, H. C. *Great Britain and the United States*. London, 1955.

16 ANDERSON, Eugene N. *The First Moroccan Crisis, 1904–1906*. Chicago, 1930.

17 BEALE, Howard K. *Theodore Roosevelt and the Rise of America to World Power*. See **27.5**.

18 BURTON, David H. "Theodore Roosevelt and Egyptian Nationalism." *Mid-Am*, XLI (1959), 88-103.

19 CAMPBELL, Alexander E. *Great Britain and the United States, 1895–1903*. London, 1960.

20 CAMPBELL, Charles S., Jr. *Anglo-American Understanding, 1898–1903*. Baltimore, 1957.

21 CAMPBELL, John P. "Taft, Roosevelt, and the Arbitration Treaties of 1911." *J Am Hist*, LIII (1966), 279-298.

22 COHEN, Naomi W. "Ambassador Strauss in Turkey, 1909–1910: A Note on Dollar Diplomacy." *Miss Val Hist Rev*, XLV (1959), 632-642.

23 DANIEL, Robert L. "The Armenian Question and American-Turkish Relations, 1914–1927." *Miss Val Hist Rev*, XLVI (1959), 252-275.

24 DAVIS, Calvin DeArmond. *The United States and the First Hague Peace Conference*. Ithaca, N.Y., 1962.

1   DENNETT, Tyler. *John Hay.* See **28.18.**

2   DENNIS, A. L. P. "John Hay." See **28.19.**

3   GELBER, Lionel M. *The Rise of Anglo-American Friendship: A Study in World Politics, 1898–1906.* London, 1936.

4   GWYNN, Stephen, ed. *The Letters and Friendships of Sir Cecil Spring-Rice.* 2 vols. Boston, 1929.

5   HALL, Luella J. "A Partnership in Peacemaking: Theodore Roosevelt and Wilhelm II." *Pac Hist Rev,* XIII (1944), 390-411.

6   HARBAUGH, William H. *Power and Responsibility.* See **6.1**

7   HEINDEL, Richard H. *The American Impact on Great Britain, 1898–1914.* Philadelphia, 1940.

8   JAMISON, Alden. "The Irish Question and American Diplomacy, 1895–1921." Doctoral dissertation, Harvard University, 1942.

9   JESSUP, Philip. *Elihu Root.* See **6.10.**

10 LEOPOLD, Richard W. *Elihu Root and the Conservative Tradition.* See **6.19.**

11 NEVINS, Allen. *Henry White: Thirty Years of American Diplomacy.* New York, 1930.

12 PERKINS, Bradford. *The Great Rapprochement: England and the United States, 1895–1914.* New York, 1968.

13 PRINGLE, Henry F. *The Life and Times of William Howard Taft.* See **7.17**

14 PRINGLE, Henry F. *Theodore Roosevelt.* See **7.18.**

15 ROOSEVELT, Theodore. *An Autobiography.* See **7.20.**

16 ROTHSTEIN, Morton. "America in the International Rivalry for the British Wheat Market, 1860–1914." *Miss Val Hist Rev,* XLVII (1960), 401-418.

17 SCHIEBER, Clara E. *The Transformation of American Sentiment toward Germany, 1870–1914.* Boston, 1923.

18 SCOTT, James Brown. "Elihu Root." See **32.9**

19 SCOTT, James Brown. *The Hague Conferences of 1899 and 1907.* Baltimore, 1909.

20 THORSON, Winston B. "American Public Opinion and the Portsmouth Peace Conference." *Am Hist Rev,* LIII (1948), 439-464.

21 VAGTS, Alfred. *Deutschland und die Vereinigten Staaten in der Weltpolitik.* 2 vols. New York, 1935.

22 VAGTS, Alfred. "Hopes and Fears of an American-German War, 1870–1915." *Pol Sci Q,* LIV (1939), 514-535; LV (1940), 53-76.

23 WRIGHT, Herbert F. "Philander C. Knox." See **32.14.**

5. *The United States and Asia*

24 BAILEY, Thomas A. "California, Japan, and the Alien Land Legislation of 1913." *Pac Hist Rev,* I (1932), 36-59.

25 BAILEY, Thomas A. "Japan's Protest Against the Annexation of Hawaii." *J Mod Hist,* III (1931), 46-61.

1   BAILEY, Thomas A. "The Root-Takahira Agreement of 1908." *Pac Hist Rev*, IX (1940), 19-36.

2   BAILEY, Thomas A. *Theodore Roosevelt and the Japanese-American Crises.* Stanford, 1934.

3   BEALE, Howard K. *Theodore Roosevelt and the Rise of America to World Power.* See **27.5**.

4   BEERS, Burton F. "Robert Lansing's Proposed Bargain with Japan." *Pac Hist Rev*, XXVI (1947), 391-400.

5   BEERS, Burton F. *Vain Endeavor: Robert Lansing's Attempts to End the American-Japanese Rivalry.* Durham, N.C., 1962.

6   BRAISTED, William R. "The Philippine Naval Base Problem, 1898–1909." *Miss Val Hist Rev*, XLI (1954), 21-40.

7   BRAISTED, William R. *The United States Navy in the Pacific, 1898–1907.* Austin, Tex., 1958.

8   BRAISTED, William R. "The United States Navy's Dilemma in the Pacific, 1906–1909." *Pac Hist Rev*, XXVI (1957), 235-244.

9   BUELL, Raymond L. "The Development of Anti-Japanese Agitation in the United States." *Pol Sci Q*, XXXVII (1922), 605-638; XXXVIII (1923), 57-81.

10   CAMERON, Meribeth E. "American Recognition Policy toward the Republic of China, 1912–1913." *Pac Hist Rev*, II (1933), 214-230.

11   CLINARD, Outten J. *Japan's Influence on American Naval Power, 1897–1917.* Berkeley, 1947.

12   COLETTA, Paola E. " 'The Most Thankless Task': Bryan and the California Alien Land Legislation." *Pac Hist Rev*, XXXVI (1967), 163-188.

13   CROLY, Herbert. *Willard Straight.* New York, 1925.

14   CURRY, Roy W. *Woodrow Wilson and Far Eastern Policy, 1913–1921.* New York, 1957.

15   CURRY, Roy W. "Woodrow Wilson and Philippine Policy." *Miss Val Hist Rev*, XLI (1954), 435-452.

16   DANIELS, Roger. *The Politics of Prejudice: The Anti-Japanese Movement in California and the Struggle for Japanese Exclusion.* Berkeley, 1962.

17   DENNETT, Tyler. *John Hay.* See **28.18**.

18   DENNETT, Tyler. *Roosevelt and the Russo-Japanese War.* Garden City, N.Y., 1925.

19   DENNIS, A. L. P. "John Hay." See **28.19**.

20   ESTHUS, Raymond A. "The Changing Concept of the Open Door, 1899–1910." *Miss Val Hist Rev*, XLVI (1959), 435-454.

21   ESTHUS, Raymond A. "The Taft-Katsura Agreement—Reality or Myth?" *J Mod Hist*, XXXI (1959), 46-51.

22   ESTHUS, Raymond A. *Theodore Roosevelt and Japan.* Seattle, 1966.

23   FIFIELD, Russell H. *Woodrow Wilson and the Far East: The Diplomacy of the Shantung Question.* New York, 1952.

24   [FULLER, Joseph V.] "William Jennings Bryan." See **31.3**.

1   GRISWOLD, A. Whitney. *The Far Eastern Policy of the United States*. New Haven, 1938.†

2   GRUNDER, Garel A. and William E. LIVEZEY. *The Philippines and the United States*. Norman, Okla., 1951.

3   HARBAUGH, William H. *Power and Responsibility*. See **6.1**.

4   HARRINGTON, Fred H. *God, Mammon, and the Japanese: Dr. Horace N. Allen and Korean-American Relations, 1884–1905*. Madison, Wis., 1946.

5   HUNTINGTON-WILSON, F. M. *Memoirs of an Ex-Diplomat*. Boston, 1945.

6   JESSUP, Philip. *Elihu Root*. See **6.10**.

7   LEOPOLD, Richard W. *Elihu Root and the Conservative Tradition*. See **6.19**.

8   LI, Tien-yi. *Woodrow Wilson's China Policy, 1913–1917*. Kansas City, Mo., 1952.

9   LINK, Arthur S. *Wilson: The New Freedom*. See **6.24**.

10   LIVERMORE, Seward W. "The American Navy as a Factor in World Politics, 1903–1913." *Am Hist Rev,* LXIII (1958), 863-879.

11   MC CORMICK, Thomas J. *China Market: America's Quest for Informal Empire, 1893–1901*. Chicago, 1967.

12   MINGER, Ralph Eldin. "Taft's Missions to Japan: A Study in Personal Diplomacy." *Pac Hist Rev,* XXX (1961), 279-294.

13   MORISON, Elting E. and John M. BLUM, eds. *The Letters of Theodore Roosevelt*. See **7.9**.

14   NEU, Charles E. "Theodore Roosevelt and American Involvement in the Far East, 1901–1909." *Pac Hist Rev,* XXXV (1966), 433-450.

15   NEU, Charles E. *An Uncertain Friendship: Theodore Roosevelt and Japan, 1906–1909*. Cambridge, Mass., 1967.

16   PRATT, Julius W. "Robert Lansing." See **32.1**

17   PRESCOTT, Francis C. "The Lansing-Ishii Agreement." Doctoral dissertation, Yale University, 1949.

18   PRINGLE, Henry F. *The Life and Times of William Howard Taft*. See **7.17**.

19   PRINGLE, Henry F. *Theodore Roosevelt*. See **7.18**.

20   REINSCH, Paul S. *An American Diplomat in China*. Garden City, N.Y., 1922.

21   REMER, C. F. *Foreign Investments in China*. New York, 1933.

22   ROOSEVELT, Theodore. *An Autobiography*. See **7.20**.

23   SANDMEYER, Elmer C. *The Anti-Chinese Movement in California*. Urbana, Ill., 1939.

24   SCOTT, James Brown. "Elihu Root." See **32.9**.

25   STEELMAN, Lala Carr. "Senator Augustus O. Bacon, Champion of Philippine Independence." *East Carolina College Publications in History,* II (1965), 91-113.

26   TATE, Merze. *The United States and the Hawaiian Kingdom: A Political History*. New Haven, 1965.

27   THORSON, Winston B. "American Public Opinion and the Portsmouth Peace Conference." See **33.20**.

28   TREAT, Payson J. *Diplomatic Relations Between the United States and Japan, 1895–1905*. Stanford, 1938.

1 TUPPER, Eleanor and George E. MC REYNOLDS. *Japan in American Public Opinion.* New York, 1937.

2 VARG, Paul A. *Missionaries, Chinese, and Diplomats.* Princeton, 1958.

3 VARG, Paul A. "The Myth of the China Market, 1890–1914."*Am Hist Rev,* LXXIII (1968), 742-758.

4 VARG, Paul A. *Open Door Diplomat: The Life of W.W. Rockhill.* Urbana, Ill., 1952.

5 VARG, Paul A. "William Woodville Rockhill and the Open Door Notes." *J Mod Hist,* XXIV (1952), 375-379.

6 VEVIER, Charles. "The Open Door: An Idea in Action, 1906–1913." *Pac Hist Rev,* XXIV (1955), 49-62.

7 VEVIER, Charles. *The United States and China, 1906–1913.* New Brunswick, N.J., 1955.

8 WHITE, John Albert. "As the Russians Saw Our China Policy." *Pac Hist Rev,* XXVI (1957), 146-160.

9 WHITE, John Albert. *The Diplomacy of the Russo–Japanese War.* Princeton, 1964.

10 WRIGHT, Herbert F. "Philander C. Knox." See **33**.23.

11 ZABRISKIE, Edward H. *American–Russian Rivalry in the Far East, 1895–1914.* Philadelphia, 1946.

6. The Road to War, 1914–1917

12 ALLEN, Howard W. "Republican Reformers and Foreign Policy, 1913–1917." *Mid-Am,* XLIV (1962), 222-229.

13 BAILEY, Thomas A. "The Sinking of the *Lusitania."* Am Hist Rev, XLI (1935), 54-73.

14 BAILEY, Thomas A. "The United States and the Blacklist during the Great War." *J Mod Hist,* VI (1934), 14-35.

15 BAILEY, Thomas A. "World War Analogues of the *Trent* Affair." *Am Hist Rev,* XXXVIII (1933), 286-290.

16 BAKER, Ray Stannard. *Woodrow Wilson: Life and Letters. See* **4**.4.

17 BERNSTORFF, Johann H. von. *My Three Years in America.* New York, 1920.

18 BETHMANN HOLLWEG, Theobald von. *Betrachtungen zum Weltkriege.* 2 vols. Berlin, 1919-1922.

19 BILLINGTON, Monroe. "The Gore Resolution of 1916." *Mid-Am,* XLVII (1965), 89-98.

20 BIRDSALL, Paul. "Neutrality and Economic Pressures, 1914–1917."*Science and Society,* III (1939), 217-228.

21 BIRNBAUM, Karl E. *Peace Moves and U-Boat Warfare.* Stockholm, 1958.

22 BRYAN, Mary B., ed. *The Memoirs of William Jennings Bryan.* See **4**.17.

23 BUCHANAN, Russell. "Theodore Roosevelt and American Neutrality, 1914–1917." *Am Hist Rev,* XLIII (1938), 775-790.

24 BUEHRIG, Edward H. "Wilson's Neutrality Re-Examined." *World Politics,* III (1950), 1-19.

1   BUEHRIG, Edward H. *Woodrow Wilson and the Balance of Power.* Bloomington, Ind., 1955.

2   CAMBON, Henri, ed. *Paul Cambon, Correspondence, 1870–1924.* 3 vols. Paris, 1940–1946.

3   CHILD, Clifton J. *The German–Americans in Politics, 1914–1917.* Madison, Wis., 1939.

4   CHURCHILL, Winston S. *The World Crisis.* 6 vols. London, 1932.

5   CRIGHTON, John C. "The *Wilhelmina:* An Adventure in the Assertion and Exercise of American Trading Rights during the World War." *Am J Int Law,* XXXIV (1940), 74-88.

6   CRONON, E. David, ed. *The Cabinet Diaries of Josephus Daniels,1913–1921.* See **5.2.**

7   CURTI, Merle E. *Bryan and World Peace.* Northampton, Mass., 1931.

8   DANIELS, Josephus. *The Wilson Era.* See **5.5.**

9   DUBIN, Martin David. "Elihu Root and the Advocacy of a League of Nations, 1914–1917." *W Pol Q,* XIX (1966), 439-455.

10 EPSTEIN, Klaus. *Matthias Erzberger and the Dilemma of German Democracy.* Princeton, 1959.

11 FISCHER, Fritz. *Germany's Aims in the First World War.* New York, 1967. (A translation of *Griff nach der Weltmach.)*

12 FULLER, Joseph V. "The Genesis of the Munitions Traffic." *J Mod Hist,* VI (1934), 280-293.

13 GERARD, James W. *My Four Years in Germany.* New York, 1917.

14 GREGORY, Ross. "A New Look at the *Dacia." J Am Hist,* LV (1968), 292-296.

15 GREW, Joseph C. *Turbulent Era: A Diplomatic Record of Forty Years, 1904–45.* 2 vols. Boston, 1952.

16 GREY, Edward (Viscount Grey of Fallodon). *Twenty-Five Years,1892–1916.* 2 vols. New York, 1925.

17 GWYNN, Stephen, ed. *The Letters and Friendships of Sir Cecil Spring-Rice.* See **33.4.**

18 HAGEDORN, Hermann. *The Bugle that Woke America.* New York, 1940.

19 HAGEDORN, Hermann. *Leonard Wood.* See **5.24.**

20 HARBAUGH, William H. "Wilson, Roosevelt, and American Interventionism, 1914–1917." Doctoral dissertation, Northwestern University, 1954.

21 HEINRICHS, Waldo H., Jr. *American Ambassador: Joseph C. Grew and the Development of the U.S. Diplomatic Tradition.* Boston, 1967.

22 HENDRICK, Burton J. *The Life and Letters of Walter H. Page.* See **6.4.**

23 HERRING, George C., Jr. "James Hay and the Preparedness Controversy, 1915–1916." *J S Hist,* XXX (1964), 383-404.

24 HIRST, David W. "German Propaganda in the United States,1914–1917." Doctoral dissertation, Northwestern University, 1962.

25 LANGER, William L. "From Isolation to Mediation." *Woodrow Wilson and the World of Today.* Ed. by Arthur P. Dudden. Philadelphia, 1957.

26 LEOPOLD, Richard W. "The Problem of American Intervention in 1917: An Historical Retrospect." *World Politics,* II (1950), 404-425.

1   LINK, Arthur S. "The Cotton Crisis, the South, and Anglo-American Diplomacy, 1914–1915." *Studies in Southern History in Memory of Albert Ray Newsome.* Ed. by J. C. Sitterson. Chapel Hill, 1957.

2   LINK, Arthur S. *Wilson: Campaigns for Progressivism and Peace, 1916–1917.* See **6.22.**

3   LINK, Arthur S. *Wilson: Confusions and Crises, 1915–1916.* See **6.23.**

4   LINK, Arthur S. *Wilson the Diplomatist.* Baltimore, 1957.†

5   LINK, Arthur S. *Wilson: The Struggle for Neutrality, 1914–1915.* See **6.26.**

6   LLOYD GEORGE, David. *The War Memoirs of David Lloyd George.* 6 vols. London, 1933–1936.

7   LOWITT, Richard. "The Armed-Ship Bill Controversy: A Legislative View." *Mid-Am,* XLVI (1964), 38-47.

8   MAY, Ernest R. "American Policy and Japan's Entrance into World War I." *Miss Val Hist Rev,* XL (1953), 279-290.

9   MAY, Ernest R. *The World War and American Isolation, 1914–1917.* Cambridge, Mass., 1959.

10 MILLIS, Walter. *Road to War: America, 1914–1917.* Boston, 1935.

11 MOONEY, Chase C. and Martha E. LAYMAN. "Some Phases of the Compulsory Military Training Movement, 1914–1920." *Miss Val Hist Rev,* XXXVIII (1952), 633-656.

12 MORRISSEY, Alice. *The American Defense of Neutral Rights, 1914–1917.* Cambridge, Mass., 1939.

13 NOTTER, Harley. *The Origins of the Foreign Policy of Woodrow Wilson.* Baltimore, 1937.

14 PALMER, Frederick. *Newton D. Baker.* See **7.15.**

15 POINCARÉ, Raymond. *Au Service de la France, Neuf Années de Souvenirs.* 10 vols. Paris, 1926–1933.

16 PRATT, Julius W. "Robert Lansing." See **32.1.**

17 RAPPAPORT, Armin. *The British Press and Wilsonian Neutrality.* Stanford, 1951.

18 READ, James Morgan. *Atrocity Propaganda, 1914–1919.* New Haven, 1941.

19 RITTER, Gerhard. *Staatskunst und Kriegshandwerk.* Vol. III. Munich, 1964.

20 SCHMITT, Bernadotte E. "American Neutrality, 1914–1917." *J Mod Hist,* VIII (1936), 200-211.

21 SEYMOUR, Charles. *American Neutrality, 1914–1917.* New Haven, 1935.

22 SEYMOUR, Charles. *The Intimate Papers of Colonel House.* See **7.25.**

23 SINEY, Marion. *The Allied Blockade of Germany, 1914–1916.* Ann Arbor, Mich., 1957.

24 SINEY, Marion. "British Negotiations with American Meat Packers, 1915–1917: A Study of Belligerent Trade Controls." *J Mod Hist,* XXIII (1951), 343-353.

25 SMITH, Daniel M. "National Interest and American Intervention, 1917: An Historiographical Appraisal." *J Am Hist,* LIII (1965), 5-24.

26 SMITH, Daniel M. *Robert Lansing and American Neutrality, 1914–1917.* Berkeley, 1958.

27 SMITH, Daniel M. "Robert Lansing and the Formulation of American Neutrality Policies, 1914–1915." *Miss Val Hist Rev,* XLIII (1956), 59-81.

1   SPINDLER, Arno. *Der Handelskrieg mit U-booten.* 3 vols. Berlin,1932–1934.

2   SQUIRES, James Duane. *British Propaganda at Home and in the United States from 1914 to 1917.* Cambridge, Mass., 1935.

3   SUTTON, Walter A. "Progressive Republican Senators and the Submarine Crisis, 1915–1916." *Mid-Am,* XLVII (1965), 75-88.

4   SYRETT, Harold C. "The Business Press and American Neutrality, 1914–1917." *Miss Val Hist Rev,* XXXII (1945), 215-230.

5   TIRPITZ, Alfred von. *Politische Dokumente von A. von Tirpitz.* 2 vols. Stuttgart and Berlin, 1924–1926.

6   VAN ALSTYNE, Richard W. "The Policy of the United States Regarding the Declaration of London, at the Outbreak of the Great War." *J Mod Hist,* VII (1935), 434-447.

7   VAN ALSTYNE, Richard W. "Private American Loans to the Allies, 1914–1916." *Pac Hist Rev,* II (1933), 180-193.

8   VIERECK, George Sylvester. *Spreading Germs of Hate.* See **24.24.**

9   WALWORTH, Arthur. *Woodrow Wilson.* See **8.11.**

10 WEINSTEIN, James. "Anti-War Sentiment and the Socialist Party." See **25.6.**

7. The First World War, Versailles, and the Great Betrayal

11 BAILEY, Thomas A. *The Policy of the United States toward the Neutrals, 1917–1918.* Baltimore, 1942.

12 BAILEY, Thomas A. *Woodrow Wilson and the Great Betrayal.* New York, 1945.†

13 BAILEY, Thomas A. *Woodrow Wilson and the Lost Peace.* New York, 1944.†

14 BAKER, Ray Stannard. *Woodrow Wilson and World Settlement.* 3 vols. Garden City, N.Y., 1922.

15 BARTLETT, Ruhl J. *The League to Enforce Peace.* Chapel Hill, 1944.

16 BIRDSALL, Paul. *Versailles Twenty Years After.* New York, 1941.

17 BUEHRIG, Edward H., ed. *Wilson's Foreign Policy in Perspective.* Bloomington, Ind., 1957.

18 BURNETT, Philip Mason. *Reparations at the Paris Peace Conference from the Standpoint of the American Delegation.* 2 vols. Cambridge, Mass., 1940.

19 CHURCHILL, Winston S. *The World Crisis.* See **37.4.**

20 COFFMAN, Edward M. *The Hilt of the Sword: The Career of Peyton C. March.* Madison, Wis., 1966.

21 CRAMER, Clarence H. *Newton D. Baker.* See **4.23.**

22 CREEL, George. *Rebel at Large.* See **4.24.**

23 CRONON, E. David, ed. *The Cabinet Diaries of Josephus Daniels, 1913–1921.* See **5.2.**

24 CURRENT, Richard N. "The United States and 'Collective Security': Notes on the History of an Idea." *Isolation and Security.* Ed. by Alexander DeConde. Durham, N.C., 1957.

1   CURRY, George. "Woodrow Wilson, Jan Smuts, and the Versailles Settlement." *Am Hist Rev*, LXVI (1961), 968-986.

2   DANIELS, Josephus. *The Wilson Era*. See **5.5**.

3   Department of the Army. *The United States Army in the World War, 1917–1919*. 13 vols. Washington, D.C., 1948.

4   EPSTEIN, Klaus. *Matthias Erzberger and the Dilemma of German Democracy*. See **37.10**.

5   FERRELL, Robert H. "Woodrow Wilson and Open Diplomacy." *Issues and Conflicts: Studies in Twentieth Century American Diplomacy*. Ed. by George L. Anderson. Lawrence, Kan., 1959.

6   FIKE, Claude E. "The Influence of the Creel Committee and the American Red Cross on Russian-American Relations, 1917–1919." *J Mod Hist*, XXXI (1959), 93-109.

7   FIKE, Claude E. "The United States and Russian Territorial Problems, 1917–1920." *Historian*, XXIV (1962), 331-346.

8   FISCHER, Fritz. *Germany's Aims in the First World War*. See **37.11**.

9   FLEMING, Denna F. *The United States and the League of Nations, 1918–1920*. New York, 1932.

10   FREIDEL, Frank B. *Over There*. Boston, 1964.

11   FROTHINGHAM, Thomas G. *The Naval History of the World War*. 3 vols. Cambridge, Mass., 1925–1926.

12   GARRATY, John A. *Henry Cabot Lodge*. See **5.10**.

13   GELFAND, Lawrence E. *The Inquiry: American Preparations for Peace, 1917–1919*. New Haven, 1963.

14   GERSON, Louis L. *Woodrow Wilson and the Rebirth of Poland, 1914–1920*. New Haven, 1953.

15   GRANTHAM, Dewey W., Jr. "The Southern Senators and the League of Nations." *N Car Hist Rev*, XXVI (1949), 187-205.

16   GRAVES, William S. *America's Siberian Adventure, 1918–1920*. New York, 1931.

17   GREW, Joseph C. *Turbulent Era*. See **37.15**.

18   GWYNN, Stephen, ed. *The Letters and Friendships of Sir Cecil Spring-Rice*. See **33.4**.

19   HARBORD, James G. *America in the World War*. Boston, 1933.

20   HELBICH, Wolfgang J. "American Liberals in the League of Nations Controversy." *Pub Opin Q*, XXXI (1967–1968), 568-596.

21   HENDRICK, Burton J. *The Life and Letters of Walter H. Page*. See **6.4**.

22   HOLT, W. Stull. *Treaties Defeated by the Senate*. Baltimore, 1933.

23   HOOVER, Herbert. *The Ordeal of Woodrow Wilson*. New York, 1958.

24   KENNAN, George F. *The Decision to Intervene*. Princeton, 1958.†

25   KENNAN, George F. *Russia Leaves the War*. Princeton, 1956.†

26   LANCASTER, James L. "The Protestant Churches and the Fight for Ratification of the Versailles Treaty." *Pub Opin Q*, XXXI (1967–1968), 597-619.

27   LANGER, William L. "Peace and the New World Order." *Woodrow Wilson and the World of Today*. Ed. by Arthur P. Duddon. Philadelphia, 1957.

1   LANGER, William L. "Woodrow Wilson: His Education in World Affairs." *Confluence,* V (1956), 183-194.

2   LANSING, Robert. *The Peace Negotiations.* Boston, 1921.

3   LANSING, Robert. *War Memoirs of Robert Lansing.* Indianapolis, 1935.

4   LASCH, Christopher. "American Intervention in Siberia: A Reinterpretation." *Pol Sci Q,* LXXVII (1962), 205-223.

5   LASCH, Christopher. *The American Liberals and the Russian Revolution.* New York, 1962.

6   LEVIN, N. Gordon, Jr. *Woodrow Wilson and World Politics: America's Response to War and Revolution.* New York, 1968.

7   LINK, Arthur S. *Wilson the Diplomatist.* See **38.4.**

8   LLOYD GEORGE, David. *The War Memoirs of David Lloyd George.* See **38.6.**

9   LOGAN, Rayford W. *The Senate and the Versailles Mandate System.* Washington, D.C., 1945.

10   LOUIS, William Roger. *Great Britain and Germany's Lost Colonies, 1914–1919.* London, 1967.

11   LOWRY, Bullitt. "Pershing and the Armistice." *J Am Hist,* LV (1968), 281-291.

12   MAMATEY, Victor S. *The United States and East Central Europe, 1914–1919.* Princeton, 1957.

13   MANTOUX, Paul. *Les délibérations du Conseil des quatre, 24 mars–28 juin 1919.* 2 vols. Paris, 1955. (For a translated edition, see John Boardman Witton, *Paris Peace Conference, 1919* [Geneva, 1964].)

14   MARTIN, Laurence W. *Peace Without Victory: Woodrow Wilson and the British Liberals.* New Haven, 1958.

15   MARTIN, Laurence W. "Woodrow Wilson's Appeals to the Peoples of Europe: British Radical Influence on the President's Strategy." *Pol Sci Q,* LXXIV (1959), 498-516.

16   MAXWELL, Kenneth R. "Irish-Americans and the Fight for Treaty Ratification." *Pub Opin Q,* XXXI (1967–1968), 620-641.

17   MAYER, Arno J. *Political Origins of the New Diplomacy, 1917–1918.* New Haven, 1959.†

18   MAYER, Arno J. *Politics and Diplomacy of Peacemaking: Containment and Counterrevolution at Versailles, 1918–1919.* New York, 1967.

19   MERRITT, Richard L. "Woodrow Wilson and the 'Great and Solemn Referendum,' 1920." *Rev Pol,* XXVII (1965), 78-104.

20   MILLER, David Hunter. *My Diary at the Conference of Paris.* 21 vols. New York, 1924.

21   MORISON, Elting E. *Admiral Sims and the Modern American Navy.* Boston, 1942.

22   MOTT, T. Bentley. *Myron T. Herrick, Friend of France.* Garden City, N.Y., 1929.

23   NICOLSON, Harold. *Peacemaking, 1919.* Boston, 1933.

24   O'GRADY, Joseph P., ed. *The Immigrants' Influence on Wilson's Peace Policies.* Lexington, Ky., 1967.

25   OSGOOD, Robert E. "Woodrow Wilson, Collective Security, and the Lessons of History." *Confluence,* V (1957), 341-354.

26   PALMER, Frederick. *Bliss, Peacemaker.* New York, 1934.

27   PALMER, Frederick. *Newton D. Baker.* See **7.15.**

1   PERKINS, Dexter. "Woodrow Wilson's Tour." *America in Crisis.* Ed. by Daniel Aaron. New York, 1952.

2   PERSHING, John J. *Final Report of General John J. Pershing.* Washington, D.C., 1919.

3   PERSHING, John J. *My Experiences in the World War.* 2 vols. New York, 1931.

4   POINCARÉ, Raymond. *Au Service de la France, Neuf Années de Souvenirs.* See 38.15.

5   PRATT, Julius W. "Robert Lansing." See 32.1.

6   RITTER, Gerhard. *Staatskunst und Kriegshandwerk.* Vol. IV. Munich, 1968.

7   RUDIN, Harry R. *Armistice, 1918.* New Haven, 1944.

8   SEYMOUR, Charles. *American Diplomacy during the World War.* Baltimore, 1934.

9   SEYMOUR, Charles. *The Intimate Papers of Colonel House.* See 7.25.

10 SIMS, William S. *The Victory at Sea.* Garden City, N.Y., 1920.

11 SNELL, John L. "Benedict XV, Wilson, Michaelis, and German Socialism." *Cath Hist Rev,* XXXVII (1951), 151-178.

12 SNELL, John L. "Wilson's Peace Program and German Socialism, January—March 1918." *Miss Val Hist Rev,* XXXVIII (1951), 187-214.

13 SPARGO, John. "Bainbridge Colby." *The American Secretaries of State and Their Diplomacy.* Ed. by Samuel Flagg Bemis. Vol. IX. New York, 1929.

14 STARTT, James D. "Early Press Reaction to Wilson's League Proposal." *Jour Q,* XXXIX (1962), 301-308.

15 STONE, Ralph A. "Two Illinois Senators Among the Irreconcilables." *Miss Val Hist Rev,* L (1963), 443-463.

16 STRAKHOVSKY, Leonid I. *American Opinion about Russia, 1917–1920.* Toronto, 1961.

17 TEMPERLEY, H. W. V., ed. *A History of the Peace Conference of Paris.* 6 vols. London, 1920–1924.

18 THOMPSON, John M. *Russia, Bolshevism, and the Versailles Peace.* Princeton, 1966.

19 TILLMAN, Seth P. *Anglo-American Relations at the Paris Peace Conference of 1919.* Princeton, 1961.

20 TRASK, David F. *The United States in the Supreme War Council.* Middletown, Conn., 1961.

21 UNTERBERGER, Betty M. *America's Siberian Expedition, 1918–1920.* Durham, N.C., 1956.

22 UNTERBERGER, Betty M. "President Wilson and the Decision to Send American Troops to Siberia." *Pac Hist Rev,* XXIV (1955), 63-74.

23 WALWORTH, Arthur. *Woodrow Wilson.* See 8.11.

24 WHITEMAN, Harold B., Jr., ed. *Letters from the Paris Peace Conference.* New Haven, 1965. (The letters of Charles Seymour.)

25 WIMER, Kurt. "Woodrow Wilson Tries Conciliation: An Effort that Failed." *Historian,* XXV (1963), 419-438.

26 WIMER, Kurt. "Woodrow Wilson's Plan for a Vote of Confidence." *Pennsylvania History,* XXVIII (1961), 2-16.

27 WIMER, Kurt. "Woodrow Wilson's Plans to Enter the League of Nations Through an Executive Agreement." *W Pol Q,* XI (1958), 800-812.

1   YATES, Louis A. R. *The United States and French Security, 1917–1921.* New York, 1957.

2   ZACHAREWICZ, Mary Misaela. "The Attitude of the Catholic Press toward the League of Nations." *Rec Am Cath Hist Soc,* LXVII (1956), 3-30, 88-104; LXVIII (1957), 46-50.

IV. The American People and Their Economic Institutions

1. General

3   ALLEN, Frederick Lewis. *The Lords of Creation.* New York, 1935.†

4   COBEN, Stanley and Forest G. HILL, eds. *American Economic History: Essays in Interpretation.* Philadelphia, 1966.†

5   COCHRAN, Thomas C. *The American Business System: A Historical Perspective, 1900–1950.* Cambridge, Mass., 1957.†

6   COCHRAN, Thomas C. and William MILLER. *The Age of Enterprise.* New York, 1942.†

7   DIAMOND, Sigmund. *The Reputation of the American Businessman.* Cambridge, Mass., 1955.

8   FAULKNER, Harold U. *The Decline of Laissez Faire, 1897–1917.* New York, 1951.

9   FRIEDMAN, Milton and Anna Jacobson SCHWARTZ. *A Monetary History of the United States, 1867–1960.* Princeton, 1963.

10   GOLDSMITH, Raymond W. *Financial Intermediaries in the American Economy since 1900.* Princeton, 1958.

11   JOHNSON, Emory R., *et al. History of Domestic and Foreign Commerce of the United States.* 2 vols. Washington, D.C., 1915.

12   KENDRICK, John W. *Productivity Trends in the United States.* Princeton, 1961.

13   KING, Willford I. *The National Income and Its Purchasing Power.* New York, 1930.

14   KING, Willford I. *The Wealth and Income of the People of the United States.* New York, 1915.

15   MITCHELL, Wesley C., *et al. Income in the United States: Its Amount and Distribution, 1909–1919.* 2 vols. New York, 1921-1922.

16   SOULE, George. *Prosperity Decade: From War to Depression, 1917–1929.* New York, 1947.†

17   WILLIAMSON, Harold F., ed. *The Growth of the American Economy.* 2nd ed. Englewood Cliffs, N.J., 1957.

2. Demographic Changes

18   BAKER, O. E. "Rural-Urban Migration and the National Welfare." *Ann Assn Am Geog,* XXIII (1933), 59-126.

19   CLARK, Earle. "Contributions to Urban Growth." *Pub Am Stat Assn,* XIV (1915), 654-670.

1 GALPIN, Charles J. and Theodore B. MANNY. *Interstate Migration among the Native White Population. . . .* Washington, D.C., 1934.

2 GILLETTE, John M. and George R. DAVIES. "Measure of Rural Migration and Other Factors of Urban Increase in the United States." *Pub Am Stat Assn,* XIV (1915), 642-653.

3 GINI, Corrado, *et al. Population.* Chicago, 1930.

4 GOODRICH, Carter, *et al. Migration and Economic Opportunity.* Philadelphia, 1936.

5 HOOVER, Edgar M., Jr. "Interstate Redistribution of Population, 1850–1940." *J Econ Hist,* I (1941), 199-205.

6 JEROME, Harry. *Migration and Business Cycles.* New York, 1926.

7 KENNEDY, Louise V. *The Negro Peasant Turns Cityward.* New York, 1930.

8 ROSSITER, William S. *Increase of Population in the United States, 1910–1920.* Washington, D.C., 1922.

9 THOMPSON, Warren S. and P. K. WHELPTON. *Population Trends in the United States.* New York, 1933.

10 THORNTHWAITE, C. Warren. *Internal Migration· in the United States.* Philadelphia, 1934.

11 WILLCOX, Walter F. *Studies in American Demography.* Ithaca, N.Y., 1940.

3. Concentration, Competition, and Public Policy

12 BERLE, Adolf A. and Gardiner C. MEANS. *The·Modern Corporation and Private Property.* New York, 1934.

13 BLAISDELL, Thomas C., Jr. *The Federal Trade Commission: An Experiment in the Control of Business.* See **2.8.**

14 BONBRIGHT, James C. and Gardiner C. MEANS. *The Holding Company.* New York, 1932.

15 BURNS, Arthur Robert. *The Decline of Competition.* New York, 1936.

16 BURNS, Arthur Robert. "The Process of Industrial Concentration." *Q J Econ,* XLVII (1933), 277-311.

17 CLARK, John Bates and John Maurice CLARK. *The Control of Trusts.* See **2.11.**

18 CLARK, John D. *The Federal Trust Policy.* See **2.12.**

19 CUSHMAN, Robert E. "Social and Economic Controls through Federal Taxation." See **2.13.**

20 DEWING, Arthur S. *Corporate Promotions and Reorganizations.* Cambridge, Mass., 1914.

21 DURAND, Edward Dana. *The Trust Problem.* Cambridge, Mass., 1915.

22 EDDY, Arthur Jerome. *The New Competition.* New York, 1912.

23 FAINSOD, Merle and Lincoln GORDON. *Government and the American Economy.* See **2.15.**

24 GASKILL, Nelson B. *The Regulation of Competition.* New York, 1936.

25 HAMILTON, Walton H. *Antitrust in Action.* Washington, D.C., 1940.

1   HENDERSON, Gerard C. *The Federal Trade Commission.* New Haven, 1925.

2   JENKS, Jeremiah Whipple and Walter E. CLARK. *The Trust Problem.* 5th ed. New York, 1929.

3   JOHNSON, Arthur M. "Antitrust in Transition, 1908: Ideal and Reality." See **17.10.**

4   JONES, Eliot. *The Trust Problem in the United States.* New York, 1923.

5   KIRSH, Benjamin S. *Trade Associations, the Legal Aspects.* New York, 1928.

6   KLEBANER, Benjamin J. "Potential Competition and the Antitrust Legislation of 1914." See **21.4.**

7   KNAUTH, Oswald Whitman. *The Policy of the United States towards Industrial Monopoly.* New York, 1914.

8   MEAD, Edward Sherwood. *Trust Finance.* New York, 1914.

9   MEYER, Balthasar Henry. *A History of the Northern Securities Case.* See **17.19.**

10 MILLS, Frederick C. *Economic Tendencies in the United States.* See **3.14.**

11 MITCHELL, Wesley C. *Business Cycles and Their Causes.* See **3.15.**

12 MOODY, John. *The Truth about the Trusts.* New York, 1904.

13 MOULTON, Harold G., *et al. Capital Expansion, Employment, and Economic Stability.* Washington, D.C., 1940.

14 National Industrial Conference Board. *Trade Associations: Their Economic Significance and Legal Status.* New York, 1925.

15 NELSON, Milton Nels. *Open Price Associations.* Urbana, Ill., 1922.

16 RATNER, Sidney. *American Taxation.* See **3.17.**

17 SCHLUTER, William C. *The Pre-War Business Cycle, 1907–1914.* New York, 1923.

18 SEAGER, Henry R. and Charles A. GULICK, Jr. *Trust and Corporation Problems.* See **3.18.**

19 SHARFMAN, I. L. "The Trade Association Movement." *Am Econ Rev, Supp,* XVI (1926).

20 STEVENS, William H. S. *Unfair Competition.* Chicago, 1917.

21 THORELLI, Hans B. *The Federal Antitrust Policy.* See **3.22.**

22 WATKINS, Myron W. *Industrial Combinations and Public Policy.* See **3.24.**

23 WILCOX, Clair. *Competition and Monopoly in American Industry.* Washington, D.C., 1940.

4. Finance Capitalism

24 ALLEN, Frederick Lewis. *The Great Pierpont Morgan.* New York, 1949.†

25 ALLEN, Frederick Lewis. *The Lords of Creation.* See **43.3.**

26 BRANDEIS, Louis D. *Other People's Money, and How the Bankers Use It.* New York, 1914.

27 CLEWS, Henry. *Fifty Years in Wall Street.* New York, 1908.

1 COREY, Lewis. *The House of Morgan.* New York, 1930.

2 DOWING, Cedric B. *Populists, Plungers, and Progressives: A Social History of Stock and Commodity Speculation, 1890–1936.* Princeton, 1965.

3 DEWING, Arthur S. *The Financial Policy of Corporations.* Rev. ed. New York, 1934.

4 EDWARDS, George W. *The Evolution of Finance Capitalism.* London, 1938.

5 GARRATY, John A. *Right-Hand Man.* See **5.11**.

6 GLASS, Carter. *An Adventure in Constructive Finance.* See **20.22**.

7 HARRIS, Seymour E. *Twenty Years of Federal Reserve Policy.* See **20.24**.

8 KUZNETZ, Simon. *Capital in the American Economy.* Princeton, 1961.

9 LAUGHLIN, J. Laurence. *The Federal Reserve Act.* See **21.5**.

10 MOODY, John. *Masters of Capital.* New Haven, 1921.

11 MYERS, Margaret G., *et al. The New York Money Market.* 4 vols. New York, 1913-1932.

12 NOYES, Alexander D. *Forty Years of American Finance, 1865–1907.* New York, 1909.

13 NOYES, Alexander D. *The War Period of American Finance, 1908–1925.* See **24.6**.

14 SEAGER, Henry R. and Charles A. GULICK. *Trust and Corporation Problems.* See **13.8**.

15 SPRAGUE, O. M. W. *History of Crises under the National Banking System.* Washington, D.C., 1910.

16 WARBURG, Paul M. *Essays on Banking Reform in the United States.* See **22.1**.

17 WARBURG, Paul M. *The Federal Reserve System.* See **22.2**.

18 WILLIS, Henry Parker. *The Federal Reserve System.* See **22.3**.

5. Manufacturing and Other Industries

19 AITKEN, Hugh G. T. *Taylorism at Watertown Arsenal: Scientific Management in Action, 1908–1915.* Cambridge, Mass., 1960.

20 ANDREWS, John B. *Phosphorus Poisoning in the Match Industry in the United States.* Washington, D.C., 1910.

21 BARITZ, Loren. *The Servants of Power: A History of the Use of Social Science in American Industry.* Middletown, Conn., 1960.†

22 BERGER, Harold and Sam H. SCHURR. *The Mining Industry: A Study of Output, Employment and Production.* New York, 1944.

23 BERGLUND, Abraham and Philip G. WRIGHT. *The Tariff on Iron and Steel.* Washington, D.C., 1929.

24 BULEY, R. Carlyle. *The Equitable Life Assurance Society of the United States.* New York, 1959.

25 CHANEY, Lucian W. and Hugh S. HANNA. *The Safety Movement in the Iron and Steel Industry in the United States.* Washington, D.C., 1918.

1   CLARK, Victor S. *History of Manufactures.* 3 vols. New York, 1929.

2   CLEMEN, Rudolf Alexander. *The American Livestock and Meat Industry.* New York, 1923.

3   COCHRAN, Thomas C. *The Pabst Brewing Company: The History of an American Business.* New York, 1948.

4   COLE, Arthur Harrison. *The American Wool Manufacture.* 2 vols. Cambridge, Mass., 1926.

5   COPELAND, Melvin Thomas. *The Cotton Manufacturing Industry of the United States.* Cambridge, Mass., 1912.

6   COPLEY, Frank Barkley. *Frederick W. Taylor.* 2 vols. New York, 1923.

7   DAY, Edmund E. and Woodlief THOMAS. *The Growth of Manufactures, 1899 to 1923.* Washington, D.C., 1928.

8   FABRICANT, Solomon. *The Output of Manufacturing Industries, 1899–1937.* New York, 1940.

9   GARRATY, John A. *Right-Hand Man.* See **5.11.**

10   GIBB, George Sweet and Evelyn H. KNOWLTON. *The Resurgent Years, 1911–1927: History of Standard Oil Company (New Jersey).* New York, 1956.

11   HABER, Samuel. *Efficiency and Uplift.* See **9.7.**

12   HAMMOND, John W. *Men and Volts: The Story of General Electric.* Philadelphia, 1941.

13   HENDRICK, Burton J. *The Life of Andrew Carnegie.* See **6.3.**

14   HIDY, Ralph W. and Muriel E. *Pioneering in Big Business, 1882–1911: History of Standard Oil Company (New Jersey).* New York, 1955.

15   HOOVER, Edgar M., Jr. *Location Theory and the Shoe and Leather Industries.* Cambridge, Mass., 1937.

16   ISE, John. *The United States Oil Policy.* See **21.1.**

17   JAMES, Marquis. *Alfred I. Du Pont: The Family Rebel.* Indianapolis, 1941.

18   KEIR, Malcolm. *Manufacturing.* New York, 1928.

19   KELLER, Morton. *The Life Insurance Enterprise, 1885–1910: A Study in the Limits of Corporate Power.* Cambridge, Mass., 1963.

20   KUBE, Harold D. and Ralph H. DANKOF. *Changes in Distribution of Manufacturing Wage Earners, 1899–1939.* Washington, D.C., 1942.

21   KUHLMANN, Charles B. *The Development of the Flour-Milling Industry in the United States.* Boston, 1929.

22   LARSON, Henrietta M. and Kenneth Wiggins PORTER. *History of Humble Oil & Refining Company: A Study in Industrial Growth.* New York, 1959.

23   LOOS, John L. *Oil on Stream! A History of Interstate Pipeline Company, 1909–1959.* Baton Rouge, 1959.

24   MC DONALD, Forrest. *Insull.* Chicago, 1962.

25   MC DONALD, Forrest. *Let There Be Light: The Electric Utility Industry in Wisconsin, 1881–1955.* Madison, Wis., 1957.

26   MC LAUGHLIN, Glenn E. *Growth of American Manufacturing Areas.* Pittsburgh, 1938.

1 MOORE, Charles W. *Timing a Century: History of the Waltham Watch Company.* Cambridge, Mass., 1945.

2 NEVINS, Allan. *Study in Power: John D. Rockefeller, Industrialist and Philanthropist.* 2 vols. New York, 1953.

3 NEWCOMER, Mabel. *The Big Business Executive.* New York, 1955.

4 O'CONNOR, Harvey. *Mellon's Millions.* New York, 1933.

5 SEVERSON, Robert F., Jr. "The American Manufacturing Frontier, 1870–1940." *Bus Hist Rev,* XXXIV (1960), 356-372.

6 STEIGERWALT, Albert K. *The National Association of Manufacturers, 1895–1914: A Study in Business Leadership.* Ann Arbor, Mich., 1964.

7 STEIGERWALT, Albert K. "The NAM and the Congressional Investigations of 1913: A Case Study in the Suppression of Evidence." *Bus Hist Rev,* XXXIV (1960), 335-344.

8 TARBELL, Ida M. *The Life of Elbert H. Gary.* New York, 1925.

9 THOMPSON, Clarence B., ed. *Scientific Management.* Cambridge, Mass., 1914.

10 THOMPSON, Tracy E. *Location of Manufactures, 1899–1929.* Washington, D.C., 1933.

11 THORP, Willard L. *The Integration of Industrial Operations.* Washington, D.C., 1924.

12 WARSHOW, Herman T., ed. *Representative Industries in the United States.* New York, 1928.

13 WOOD, Norman J. "Industrial Relations Policies of American Management, 1900–1933." *Bus Hist Rev,* XXXIV (1960), 403-420.

6. Transportation

14 AGG, Thomas R. and John E. BRINDLEY. *Highway Administration and Finance.* New York, 1927.

15 BONBRIGHT, James C. *Railroad Capitalization.* New York, 1920.

16 CAMPBELL, E. G. *The Reorganization of the American Railroad System, 1893–1900.* New York, 1938.

17 DEARING, Charles L. *American Highway Policy.* Washington, D.C., 1941.

18 DIXON, Frank Haigh. *Railroads and Government: Their Relations in the United States, 1910–1921.* New York, 1922.

19 DOSTER, James F. *Railroads in Alabama Politics, 1875–1914.* University, Ala., 1957.

20 FERGUSON, Maxwell. *State Regulation of Railroads in the South.* New York, 1916.

21 HARBESON, Robert W. "Railroads and Regulation, 1877–1916: Conspiracy or Public Interest?" See **3.3.**

22 HUTCHINS, John G. B. *The American Maritime Industries and Public Policy, 1789–1914.* Cambridge, Mass., 1941.

23 KEMBLE, John Haskell. "The Transpacific Railroads, 1869–1915." *Pac Hist Rev,* XVIII (1949), 331-344.

24 KENNAN, George. *E. H. Harriman.* 2 vols. Boston, 1922.

1 KENNEDY, Edward D. *The Automobile Industry.* New York, 1941.

2 KOLKO, Gabriel. *Railroads and Regulation.* See **3.10.**

3 LOCKLIN, D. Philip. *Economics of Transportation.* Chicago, 1935.

4 LOWITT, Richard. "George W. Norris, James J. Hill, and the Railroad Rate Bill." See **17.16.**

5 MASON, Edward S. *The Street Railway in Massachusetts.* Cambridge, Mass., 1932.

6 MILLER, Sidney L. *Railway Transportation.* Chicago, 1925.

7 MOULTON, Harold G. *Waterways versus Railways.* Rev. ed. Boston, 1926.

8 MOULTON, Harold G., *et al. The American Transportation Problem.* Washington, D.C., 1933.

9 NEVINS, Allan. *Ford, the Times, the Man, the Company.* New York, 1954.

10 PYLE, Joseph G. *The Life of James J. Hill.* 2 vols. Garden City, N.Y., 1917.

11 RIPLEY, William Z. *Railroads: Finance & Organization.* New York, 1920.

12 RIPLEY, William Z. *Railroads: Rates and Regulation.* New York, 1912.

13 SCOTT, Roy V. "American Railroads and Agricultural Extension, 1900–1914: A Study in Railway Developmental Techniques." *Bus Hist Rev,* XXXIX (1965), 74-98.

14 SELTZER, Lawrence H. *A Financial History of the American Automobile Industry.* Boston, 1928.

15 SHARFMAN, I. L. *The American Railroad Problem.* New York, 1921.

16 SHARFMAN, I. L. *The Interstate Commerce Commission.* See **3.19.**

17 STAPLES, Henry L. and Alpheus T. MASON. *The Fall of a Railroad Empire.* See **11.21.**

18 SWARD, Keith T. *The Legend of Henry Ford.* New York, 1948.

19 WILCOX, Delos F. *Analysis of the Electric Railway Problem.* New York, 1921.

20 WILCOX, Delos F. *Municipal Franchises.* 2 vols. Rochester, 1910.

21 ZEIS, Paul M. *American Shipping Policy.* Princeton, 1938.

7. *Agriculture*

22 BAILEY, Joseph C. *Seaman A. Knapp, Schoolmaster of American Agriculture.* New York, 1945.

23 BAILEY, Liberty Hyde, ed. *Cyclopedea of American Agriculture.* 4 vols. New York, 1907–1909.

24 BARGER, Harold and Hans H. LANDSBERG. *American Agriculture, 1899–1939.* New York, 1942.

25 BENEDICT, Murray R. *Farm Policies of the United States, 1790–1950.* New York, 1953.

1   BOGUE, Allan G. *Money at Interest: The Farm Mortgage on the Middle Border.* Ithaca, N.Y., 1955.

2   GAUS, John M. and Leon O. WOLCOTT. *Public Administration and the United States Department of Agriculture.* Chicago, 1940.

3   GOLDENWEISER, Emanuel A. and Leon E. TRUESDALE. *Farm Tenancy in the United States.* Washington, D.C., 1924.

4   HARDING, T. Swann. *Two Blades of Grass: A History of Scientific Development in the U.S. Department of Agriculture.* Norman, Okla., 1947.

5   HARGREAVES, Mary Wilma M. *Dry Farming in the Northern Great Plains, 1900–1925.* Cambridge, Mass., 1957.

6   JAMIESON, Stuart. *Labor Unionism in American Agriculture.* See **15.11**.

7   NOURSE, Edwin G., *et al. American Agriculture and the European Market.* New York, 1924.

8   SALOUTOS, Theodore. *Farmer Movements in the South, 1865–1933.* See **15.13**.

9   SALOUTOS, Theodore and John D. HICKS. *Agricultural Discontent in the Middle West, 1900–1939.* See **15.16**.

10   SHANNON, Fred A. "The Status of the Midwestern Farmer in 1900." See **15.17**.

11   SHEPARDSON, Whitney H. *Agricultural Education in the United States.* New York, 1929.

12   THOMPSON, Carl W. *Cost and Sources of Farm-Mortgage Loans in the United States.* Washington, D.C., 1916.

13   TRUE, Alfred C. *A History of Agricultural Education in the United States, 1785–1925.* Washington, D.C., 1929.

14   TRUE, Alfred C. *A History of Agricultural Experimentation and Research in the United States, 1607–1925.* Washington, D.C., 1937.

15   TRUESDALE, Leon E. *Farm Population of the United States.* Washington, D.C., 1926.

8. Research and Technology

16   EPSTEIN, Ralph C. "Industrial Invention: Heroic or Systematic?" *Q J Econ.* XL (1926), 232-272.

17   FLINN, Alfred D. *Research Laboratories in Industrial Establishments of the United States.* Washington, D.C., 1920.

18   HAMILTON, Walton H. *Patents and Free Enterprise.* Washington, D.C., 1941.

19   JEROME, Harry. *Mechanization in Industry.* New York, 1934.

20   JOSEPHSON, Matthew. *Edison.* New York, 1959.

21   LORWIN, Lewis L. and John M. BLAIR. *Technology in Our Economy.* Washington, D.C., 1941.

22   OLIVER, John W. *History of American Technology.* New York 1956.

23   SILK, Leonard S. *The Research Revolution.* New York, 1960.†

9. Labor

1 ADAMIC, Louis. *Dynamite: The Story of Class Violence in America.* New York, 1931.

2 ADAMS, Graham, Jr. *Age of Industrial Violence, 1910–1915.* See **16.16**.

3 ANDERSON, H. Dewey and Percy E. DAVIDSON. *Occupational Trends in the United States.* Stanford, 1940.

4 BABSON, Roger W. *W. B. Wilson and the Department of Labor.* See **18.18**.

5 BERMAN, Edward. *Labor and the Sherman Act.* New York, 1930.

6 BERMAN, Edward. *Labor Disputes and the President of the United States.* New York, 1924.

7 BING, Alexander M. *War-Time Strikes and Their Adjustment.* See **22.12**.

8 BRANDEIS, Elizabeth. "Labor Legislation." See **2.9**.

9 BRISSENDEN, Paul F. *Earnings of Factory Workers, 1899–1927.* Washington, D.C., 1929.

10 BRISSENDEN, Paul F. *The I.W.W.* See **26.15**.

11 BRODY, David. *Labor in Crisis.* See **22.15**.

12 BRODY, David. *Steelworkers in America: The Nonunion Era.* Cambridge, Mass., 1960.

13 BUDER, Stanley. *Pullman: An Experiment in Industrial Order and Community Planning, 1880–1930.* New York, 1967.

14 CHAPIN, Robert C. *The Standard of Living among Workingmen's Families in New York City.* New York, 1909.

15 COOMBS, Whitney. *The Wages of Unskilled Labor in Manufacturing Industries in the United States, 1890–1924.* New York, 1926.

16 CRONIN, Bernard C. *Father Yorke and the Labor Movement in San Francisco, 1900–1910.* Washington, D.C., 1943.

17 DAVIDSON, Elizabeth H. *Child Labor Legislation in the Southern Textile States.* See **12.20**.

18 DERBER, Milton. "The Idea of Industrial Democracy in America, 1898–1915." See **13.1**.

19 DOUGLAS, Paul H. *American Apprenticeship and Industrial Education.* New York, 1921.

20 DOUGLAS, Paul H. *Real Wages in the United States, 1890–1926.* Boston, 1930.

21 DOUGLAS, Paul H. and Aaron DIRECTOR. *The Problem of Unemployment.* New York, 1931.

22 DUBOFSKY, Melvyn. "Organized Labor and the Immigrant in New York City, 1900–1918." *Lab Hist,* II (1961), 182-201.

23 EASTMAN, Crystal. *Work-Accidents and the Law.* See **13.2**.

24 FABRICANT, Solomon. *Employment in Manufacturing, 1899–1939.* New York, 1942.

25 FAULKNER, Harold U. and Mark STARR. *Labor in America.* New York, 1944.

1 FOERSTER, Robert F. and Else H. DIETEL. *Employee Stock Ownership in the United States.* Princeton, 1929.

2 FONER, Philip S. *History of the Labour Movement in the United States.* 4 vols. New York, 1947-

3 FRANKFURTER, Felix and N. GREENE. *The Labor Injunction.* New York, 1930.

4 FRENCH, Carroll E. *The Shop Committee in the United States.* Baltimore, 1923.

5 GARRATY, John A. "The United States Steel Corporation versus Labor: The Early years." *Lab Hist,* I (1960), 3-38.

6 GLUCK, Elsie. *John Mitchell, Miner.* New York, 1929.

7 GOMPERS, Samuel. *Seventy Years of Life and Labor.* See **5.19.**

8 GREEN, Marguerite. *The National Civic Federation and the American Labor Movement, 1900–1925.* See **3.2.**

9 GREGORY, Charles O. *Labor and the Law.* New York, 1946.

10 HANSEN, Alvin H. "Industrial Class Alignments in the United States." *Pub Am Stat Assn,* XVII (1920), 417-425.

11 HANSEN, Alvin H. "Industrial Classes in the United States in 1920." *J Am Stat Assn,* XVIII (1922), 503-506.

12 HILL, Joseph A. *Women in Gainful Occupation, 1870–1920.* Washington, D.C., 1929.

13 HOHMAN, Elmo Paul. "Maritime Labour in the United States: The Seamen's Act and Its Historical Background." See **20.25.**

14 HOHMAN, Elmo Paul. "Maritime Labour in the United States: Since the Seamen's Act." *Int Lab Rev,* XXXVIII (1938), 376-403.

15 Interchurch World Movement of North America. *Report on the Steel Strike of 1919.* See **23.14.**

16 KARSON, Marc. *American Labor Unions and Politics, 1900–1918.* See **3.9.**

17 KELLOGG, Paul Underwood, ed. *The Pittsburgh Survey.* See **9.13.**

18 KUTLER, Stanley I. "Labor, the Clayton Act, and the Supreme Court." See **26.1.**

19 LAHNE, Herbert J. *The Cotton Mill Worker.* New York, 1944.

20 LANFEAR, Vincent W. *Business Fluctuations and the American Labor Movement, 1915–1922.* New York, 1924.

21 LATIMER, Murray W. *Industrial Pensions Systems in the United States.* 2 vols. New York, 1932.

22 LAUCK, W. Jett and Edgar SYDENSTRICKER. *Condition of Labor in American Industries.* New York, 1917.

23 LEIBY, James. *Carroll Wright and Labor Reform: The Origin of Labor Statistics.* Cambridge, Mass., 1960.

24 LESCOHIER, Don D. *The Labor Market.* New York, 1919.

25 LESCOHIER, Don D. "Working Conditions." See **3.12.**

26 LEVINE, Daniel. "Gompers and Racism: Strategy of Limited Objectives." *Mid-Am,* XLIII (1961), 106-113.

27 LIEBERMAN, Elias. *Unions Before the Bar.* New York, 1950.†

1 LOMBARDI, John. *Labor's Voice in the Cabinet: A History of the Department of Labor from Its Origin to 1921.* New York, 1942.

2 LORWIN, Lewis L. *The American Federation of Labor.* Washington, D.C., 1933.

3 MANDEL, Bernard. *Samuel Gompers.* See 7.2.

4 MANDEL, Bernard. "Samuel Gompers and the Negro Workers, 1886–1914." *J Neg Hist,* XL (1955), 34-60.

5 MASON, Alpheus T. *Organized Labor and the Law.* Durham, N.C., 1925.

6 MORE, Louise B. *Wage-Earners' Budgets.* New York, 1907.

7 MURRAY, Robert K. "Public Opinion, Labor, and the Clayton Act." See 21.15.

8 NADWORTHY, Milton J. *Scientific Management and the Unions, 1900–1932.* Cambridge, Mass., 1955.

9 NASH, Gerald D. "Franklin D. Roosevelt and Labor: The World War I Origins of the Early New Deal Policy." See 24.4.

10 PELLING, Henry. *American Labor.* Chicago, 1960.†

11 PERLMAN, Mark. *Labor Union Theories in America: Background and Development.* Evanston, Ill., 1958.

12 PERLMAN, Selig. *A History of Trade Unionism in the United States.* New York, 1922.

13 PERLMAN, Selig and Philip TAFT. "Labor Movements, 1896–1932." See 3.16.

14 RAYBACK, Joseph G. *A History of American Labor.* New York, 1959.†

15 REED, Louis S. *The Labor Philosophy of Samuel Gompers.* New York, 1930.

16 REES, Albert. *Real Wages in Manufacturing, 1890–1914.* Princeton, 1961.

17 SAXTON, Alexander. "San Francisco Labor and the Populist and Progressive Insurgencies." See 11.18.

18 SCHEINBERG, Stephen J. "Theodore Roosevelt and the A. F. of L.'s Entry into Politics, 1906–1908." See 18.6.

19 SEIDMAN, Joel. *The Needle Trades.* New York, 1942.

20 SELEKMAN, Ben M. and Mary VAN KLEECK. *Employees' Representation in Coal Mines.* New York, 1924.

21 SMITH, Darrell Hevenor. *The United States Employment Service.* Baltimore, 1932.

22 SMITH, John S. "Organized Labor and Government in the Wilson Era, 1913–1921: Some Conclusions." See 20.10.

23 STEWART, Bryce M., *et al. Unemployment Benefits in the United States.* New York, 1930.

24 SUFFERN, Arthur E. *Conciliation and Arbitration in the Coal Industry of America.* Boston, 1915.

25 TAFT, Philip. *The A. F. of L. in the Time of Gompers.* New York, 1957.

26 TAFT, Philip. "The Federal Trials of the IWW." See 24.20.

1 TAFT, Philip. "The I.W.W. in the Grain Belt." *Lab Hist,* I (1960), 53-67.

2 TAFT, Philip. *Organized Labor in American History.* New York, 1964.

3 TAYLOR, Albion Guilford. *Labor Policies of the National Association of Manufacturers.* Urbana, Ill., 1928.

4 TOLMAN, William H. *Social Engineering.* New York, 1909.

5 TYLER, Robert L. "The I.W.W. and the West." *Am Q,* XII (1960), 175-187.

6 WAKSTEIN, Allen M. "The Origins of the Open-Shop Movement, 1919-1920." *J Am Hist,* LI (1964), 460-475.

7 WATKINS, Gordon S. *Labor Problems and Labor Administration in the United States during the World War.* See **25.3.**

8 WEINTRAUB, Hyman. *Andrew Furuseth: Emancipator of the Seamen.* Berkeley, 1959.

9 WHELPTON, P. K. "Occupational Groups in the United States." *J Am Stat Assn,* XXI (1925), 335-343.

10 WITTE, Edwin E. *The Government in Labor Disputes.* New York, 1932.

11 WOLMAN, Leo. *The Boycott in American Trade Unions.* Baltimore, 1916.

12 WOLMAN, Leo. *The Growth of American Trade Unions, 1880–1923.* New York, 1924.

13 WOODBURY, Robert M. *Workers' Health and Safety.* New York, 1927.

14 YELLEN, Samuel. *American Labor Struggles.* New York, 1936.

15 YELLOWITZ, Irwin. *Labor and the Progressive Movement in New York City, 1897–1916.* See **12.9.**

10. Immigration

16 ADAMIC, Louis. *From Many Lands.* New York, 1940.

17 ADAMIC, Louis. *A Nation of Nations.* New York, 1945.

18 BABCOCK, Kendric C. *The Scandinavian Element in the United States.* Urbana, Ill., 1914.

19 BARRY, Colman J. *The Catholic Church and German Americans.* Milwaukee, 1953.

20 BERNARD, William S., ed. *American Immigration Policy: A Reappraisal.* New York, 1950.

21 BERTHOFF, Rowland T. *British Immigrants in Industrial America, 1790–1950.* Cambridge, Mass., 1953.

22 BERTHOFF, Rowland T. "Southern Attitudes Toward Immigration, 1865–1914." *J S Hist,* XVII (1951), 328-360.

23 BOWERS, David F., ed. *Foreign Influences in American Life: Essays and Critical Bibliographies.* Princeton, 1944.†

24 CARPENTER, Niles. *Immigrants and Their Children, 1920.* Washington, D.C., 1927.

25 CHILD, Clifton J. *The German-Americans in Politics, 1914–1917.* See **37.3.**

1 COMMONS, John R. *Races and Immigrants in America*. New York, 1907.

2 CURTI, Merle E. and Kendall BIRR. "The Immigrant and the American Image in Europe, 1860–1914." *Miss Val Hist Rev*, XXXVII (1950), 203-230.

3 DANIELS, Roger. *The Politics of Prejudice*. See **34.16**.

4 FAIRCHILD, Henry Pratt. "The Literacy Test and Its Making." *Q J Econ*, XXXI (1917), 447-460.

5 FOERSTER, Robert F. *The Italian Immigration of Our Times. Harvard University Economic Studies*, XX (1919).

6 GARIS, Roy L. *Immigration Restriction*. New York, 1927.

7 GORDON, Milton M. "Assimilation in America: Theory and Reality." *Daedalus*, XC (1961), 263-285.

8 HANDLIN, Oscar. *The American People in the Twentieth Century*. Cambridge, Mass., 1954.†

9 HANDLIN, Oscar. "American Views of the Jew at the Opening of the Twentieth Century." *Pub Am Jew Hist Soc*, XL (1951), 323-344.

10 HANDLIN, Oscar. *Race and Nationality in American Life*. New York, 1957.†

11 HANDLIN, Oscar. *The Uprooted*. Boston, 1951.†

12 HANSEN, Marcus L. *The Immigrant in American History*. Cambridge, Mass., 1940.†

13 HANSEN, Marcus L. *The Mingling of Canadian and American Peoples*. New Haven, 1940.

14 HEALD, Morrell. "Business Attitudes Toward European Immigration, 1880–1900." *J Econ Hist*, XIII (1953), 291-304.

15 HIGHAM, John. *Strangers in the Land*. See **3.6**.

16 HOGLUND, A. William. *Finnish Immigrants in America, 1880–1920*. Madison, Wis., 1960.

17 ICHIHASHI, Yamato. *Japanese in the United States*. Stanford, 1932.

18 JENKS, Jeremiah W. and W. Jett LAUCK. *The Immigrant Problem*. 5th ed. New York, 1922.

19 JOHNSON, Stanley C. *A History of Immigration from the United Kingdom to North America, 1763–1912*. London, 1913.

20 JONES, Maldwyn Allen. *American Immigration*. Chicago, 1960.†

21 LEISERSON, William M. *Adjusting Immigrant and Industry*. New York, 1924.

22 MATTHEWS, Fred H. "White Community and 'Yellow Peril.' " *Miss Val Hist Rev*, L (1964), 612-633.

23 MILLER, Herbert A. *The School and the Immigrant*. Cleveland, 1916.

24 MILLIS, Harry A. *The Japanese Problem in the United States*. New York, 1915.

25 PARK, Robert E. and Herbert A. MILLER. *Old World Traits Transplanted*. New York, 1921.

26 SALOUTOS, Theodore. *The Greeks in the United States*. Cambridge, Mass., 1964.

1   SALOUTOS, Theodore. *They Remember America: The Story of the Repatriated Greek-Americans.* Berkeley, 1956.

2   SMITH, William Carlson. *Americans in the Making: The Natural History of the Assimilation of Immigrants.* New York, 1939.

3   STEPHENSON, George M. *A History of American Immigration, 1820–1924.* Boston, 1926.

4   TAYLOR, Joseph Henry. "The Restriction of European Immigration, 1890–1924." Doctoral dissertation, University of California, 1936.

5   THOMAS, William I. and Florian ZNANIECKI. *The Polish Peasant in Europe and America.* 2 vols. New York, 1927.

6   VECOLI, Rudolph J. "Cantadini in Chicago: A Critique of the Uprooted." *J Am Hist,* LI (1964), 404-417.

7   WILLCOX, Walter F. "The Distribution of Immigrants in the United States." *Q J Econ,* XX (1906), 523-546.

8   WITTKE, Carl. *The German-Language Press in America.* Lexington, Ky., 1957.

9   WITTKE, Carl. *The Irish in America.* Baton Rouge, 1956.

10 WITTKE, Carl. *We Who Built America.* Rev. ed. Cleveland, 1964.†

11 WOOFTER, Thomas J. *Races and Ethnic Groups in American Life.* New York, 1933.

V. Social and Intellectual Main Currents in American Life

1. Social Trends and Changes

12 ATHERTON, Lewis E. *Main Street or the Middle Border.* Bloomington, Ind., 1954.†

13 BABER, Ray Erwin and Edward Alsworth ROSS. *Changes in Size of American Families in One Generation.* Madison, Wis., 1924.

14 BRECKINRIDGE, Sophonisba. *Women in the Twentieth Century.* New York, 1933.

15 BUSBEY, Katherine G. *Home Life in America.* New York, 1910.

16 DULLES, Foster Rhea. *America Learns to Play.* New York, 1940.†

17 HALL, Frederick S. and Elisabeth W. BROOKE. *American Marriage Laws.* New York, 1919.

18 LORD, Walter. *The Good Years: From 1900 to the First World War.* New York, 1960.†

19 LOU, Herbert H. *Juvenile Courts in the United States.* Chapel Hill, 1927.

20 MANGOLD, George B. *Problems of Child Welfare.* New York, 1914.

21 MAY, Henry F. *The End of American Innocence: A Study of the First Years of Our Own Time, 1912–1917.* New York, 1959.†

22 MC GOVERN, James R. "The American Woman's Pre-World War I Freedom in Manners and Morals." *J Am Hist,* LV (1968), 315-333.

23 MORRIS, Lloyd R. *Postscript to Yesterday: American Life and Thought, 1896–1946.* New York, 1947.

1   O'NEILL, William L. *Divorce in the Progressive Era.* New Haven, 1967.

2   O'NEILL, William L. "Divorce in the Progressive Era." *Am Q,* XVII (1965), 203-217.

3   POTTER, David M. *People of Plenty.* Chicago, 1954.†

4   SMUTS, Robert W. *Women and Work in America.* New York, 1959.

5   STIGLER, George J. *Domestic Servants in the United States, 1900–1940.* New York, 1946.

6   THOMAS, William I. and Florian ZNANIECKI. *The Polish Peasant in Europe and America.* See **56.5.**

2. Currents of American Thought

7   AARON, Daniel. *Men of Good Hope.* See **15.20.**

8   ADAMS, Henry. *The Education of Henry Adams.* New York, 1918.†

9   BARKER, Charles A. *Henry George.* See **4.7.**

10 CARGILL, Oscar. *Intellectual America.* New York, 1941.†

11 COMMAGER, Henry S. *The American Mind.* See **15.21.**

12 CURTI, Merle E. *The Growth of American Thought.* See. **15.22.**

13 DORFMAN, Joseph. *The Economic Mind in American Civilization.* See **16.1.**

14 DORFMAN, Joseph. *Thorstein Veblen and His America.* See **16.2.**

15 EKIRCH, Arthur A., Jr. *The Decline of American Liberalism.* New York, 1955.

16 FORD, Worthington C., ed. *Letters of Henry Adams, 1892–1918.* Boston, 1938.

17 FOX, Daniel M. *Discovery of Abundance.* See. **16.4**

18 GABRIEL, Ralph H. *The Course of American Democratic Thought.* See **16.5.**

19 HOFSTADTER, Richard. *Social Darwinism in American Thought, 1860–1915.* Philadelphia, 1944.†

20 HOOK, Sidney. *John Dewey.* See **16.8.**

21 JOOST, Nicholas. *Years of Transition,* The Dial, *1912–1920.* Barre, 1967.

22 MAY, Henry. "The Rebellion of the Intellectuals, 1912–1917." *Am Q,* VIII (1956), 114-126.

23 MC CLOSKEY, Robert Green. *American Conservatism in the Age of Enterprise: A Study of William Graham Sumner, Stephen J. Field, and Andrew Carnegie.* Cambridge, Mass., 1951.†

24 PERRY, Ralph Barton. *The Thought and Character of William James.* 2 vols. Boston, 1935. (A condensed version is available in paperback.)

25 SCHNEIDER, Herbert W. *A History of American Philosophy.* 2nd ed. New York, 1963.†

26 WHITE, Morton. *Social Thought in America.* See **16.15.**

3. Education

1 BECK, Holmes. "American Progressive Education, 1875–1930." Doctoral dissertation, Yale University, 1941.

2 BURNS, Edward McNall. *David Starr Jordan.* Stanford, 1953.

3 BUTLER, Nicholas Murray. *Across the Busy Years.* 2 vols. New York, 1939–1940.

4 BUTTS, R. Freeman and Lawrence A. CREMIN. *A History of Education in American Culture.* New York, 1953.

5 CREMIN, Lawrence A. *The Transformation of the School: Progressivism in American Education, 1876–1957.* New York, 1961.†

6 CUBBERLY, Ellwood P. *Changing Conceptions of Education.* Boston, 1909.

7 CUBBERLY, Ellwood P. *Public Education in the United States.* Boston, 1919.

8 CURTI, Merle E. "The American Scholar in Three Wars." *J Hist Ideas,* III (1942), 241-264.

9 CURTI, Merle E. *The Social Ideas of American Educators.* New York, 1935.†

10 CURTI, Merle E. and Vernon CARSTENSEN. *The University of Wisconsin: A History, 1848–1925.* Madison, Wis., 1949.

11 DABNEY, Charles William. *Universal Education in the South.* 2 vols. Chapel Hill, 1936.

12 FRENCH, John C. *A History of the University Founded by Johns Hopkins.* Baltimore, 1946.

13 HAWKINS, Hugh. "Charles W. Eliot, University Reform and Religious Faith in America, 1869–1909." *J Am Hist,* LI (1964), 191-213.

14 HERBST, Jurgen. *The German Historical School in American Scholarship: A Study in the Transfer of Culture.* Ithaca, N.Y., 1965.

15 HOLT, W. Stull, ed. *Historical Scholarship in the United States, 1876–1901: As Revealed in the Correspondence of Herbert B. Adams.* Baltimore, 1938.

16 HOOK, Sidney. *John Dewey.* See **16.8**.

17 KANDEL, I. L. *American Education in the Twentieth Century.* Cambridge, Mass., 1957.

18 KANDEL, I. L., ed. *Twenty-Five Years of American Education.* New York, 1931.

19 KNIGHT, Edgar W. *Fifty Years of American Education, 1900–1950.* New York, 1952.

20 MIMS, Edwin. *Chancellor Kirkland of Vanderbilt.* Nashville, Tenn., 1940.

21 MOORE, Ernest Carroll. *Fifty Years of American Education.* Boston, 1917.

22 MORISON, Samuel E., ed. *The Development of Harvard University since the Inauguration of President Eliot, 1869–1929.* Cambridge, Mass., 1930.

23 NOBLE, Stuart G. *A History of American Education.* New York, 1953.

1 OSBURN, W. J. *Foreign Criticisms of American Education.* Washington, D.C., 1922.

2 PIERSON, George Wilson. *Yale College: An Educational History, 1871–1921.* New Haven, 1952.

3 ROSSI, Peter H. and Alice S. "Some Effects of Parochial-School Education in America." *Daedalus*, XC (1961), 300-328.

4 RUGG, Harold. *Foundations for American Education.* Yonkers-on-Hudson, N.Y., 1947.

5 SCHILPP, Paul Arthur, ed. *The Philosophy of John Dewey.* Evanston, Ill., 1939.

6 SIZER, Theodore R. *Secondary Schools at the Turn of the Century.* New Haven, 1964.

7 VAN TASSEL, David D. "The American Historical Association and the South, 1884–1913." *J S Hist*, XXIII (1957), 465-482.

8 VEYSEY, Laurence R. *The Emergence of the American University.* Chicago, 1965.

9 WILSON, Louis R. *The University of North Carolina, 1900–1930: The Making of a Modern University.* Chapel Hill, 1957.

10 YEOMANS, Henry A. *Abbott Lawrence Lowell, 1856–1943.* Cambridge, Mass., 1948.

4. Science, Medicine, and Public Health

11 CLAPESATTLE, Helen. *The Doctors Mayo.* Minneapolis, 1941.†

12 DE KRUIF, Paul. *Microbe Hunters.* New York, 1926.†

13 DEUTSCH, Albert. *The Mentally Ill in America: A History of Their Care and Treatment from Colonial Times.* Rev. ed. New York, 1946.

14 DUPREE, A. Hunter, ed. *Science and the Emergence of Modern America, 1865–1916.* Chicago, 1963.†

15 DUPREE, A. Hunter. *Science in the Federal Government: A History of Policies and Activities to 1940.* Cambridge, Mass., 1957.

16 FLEMING, Donald. *William H. Welch and the Rise of Modern Medicine.* Boston, 1954.

17 FLEXNER, Simon and J. T. *William Henry Welch and the Heroic Age of American Medicine.* New York, 1941.

18 HARROW, Benjamin. *Vitamins.* New York, 1921.

19 LEIGH, Robert D. *Federal Health Administration.* New York, 1927.

20 ROBERTS, Mary M. *American Nursing: History and Interpretation.* New York, 1954.

21 RODGERS, Andrew Denny, III. *Liberty Hyde Bailey.* Princeton, 1949.

22 SHRYOCK, Richard H. *American Medical Research.* New York, 1947.

23 SHRYOCK, Richard H. *The Development of Modern Medicine.* New York, 1947.

24 TOBEY, James A. *The National Government and Public Health.* Baltimore, 1926.

5. Religion

1   ABRAMS, Ray H. *Preachers Present Arms.* See **22.5**.

2   ABELL, Aaron I. *American Catholicism and Social Action.* See **13.24**.

3   ABELL, Aaron I. "The Religious Aspect of American Life." *Rev Pol,* XXI (1959), 24-52.

4   ABELL, Aaron I. *The Urban Impact on American Protestantism, 1865–1900.* See **13.25**.

5   ARMSTRONG, Maurice W., *et al.,* eds. *The Presbyterian Enterprise: Sources of American Presbyterian History.* Philadelphia, 1956.

6   BAILEY, Kenneth K. *Southern White Protestantism in the Twentieth Century.* New York, 1964.

7   BARKER, John Marshall. *The Social Gospel and the New Era.* See **13.26**.

8   BARRY, Colman J. *The Catholic Church and German-Americans.* See **54.19**.

9   BRAUER, Jerald C. *Protestantism in America.* Rev. ed. Philadelphia, 1966.

10   ELLIS, John Tracy. *American Catholicism.* Chicago, 1956.†

11   ELLIS, John Tracy. *The Life of James Cardinal Gibbons.* 2 vols. Milwaukee, 1952.

12   FURNISS, Norman F. *The Fundamentalist Controversy, 1918–1931.* New Haven, 1954.

13   GAUSTAD, Edwin Scott. *A Religious History of America.* New York, 1967.

14   GLAZER, Nathan. *American Judaism.* Chicago, 1957.†

15   HANDY, Robert T. "Christianity and Socialism in America, 1900–1920." See **26.18**.

16   HERBERG, Will. *Protestant, Catholic, Jew.* Garden City, N.Y., 1955.†

17   HOPKINS, Charles H. *History of the Y.M.C.A. in North America.* New York, 1951.

18   HOPKINS, Charles H. *The Rise of the Social Gospel in American Protestantism, 1865–1915.* See **14.1**.

19   HUDSON, Winthrop S. *American Protestantism.* Chicago, 1961.†

20   KNOX, Israel. *Rabbi in America: The Story of Isaac M. Wise.* Boston, 1957.

21   LANKFORD, John E. "The Impact of the New Era Movement on the Presbyterian Church in the United States of America, 1918–1925." *J Presby Hist,* XL (1962), 213-224.

22   MAY, Henry F. *Protestant Churches and Industrial America.* See **14.2**.

23   MAYNARD, Theodore. *The Story of American Catholicism.* New York, 1943.†

24   MC AVOY, Thomas T. "The Catholic Minority after the Americanist Controversy, 1899–1917: A Survey." *Rev Pol,* XXI (1959), 53-82.

25   MILLER, Robert Moats. "Methodism and American Society, 1900–1939." See **14.3**.

26   MOYNIHAN, James H. *The Life of Archbishop John Ireland.* New York, 1953.

27   OLMSTEAD, Clifton E. *History of Religion in the United States.* Englewood Cliffs, N.J., 1960.

1   RAUSCHENBUSH, Walter. *Christianity and the Social Crisis.* See **14.5.**

2   RAUSCHENBUSH, Walter. *A Theology for the Social Gospel.* See **14.6.**

3   SAPPINGTON, Roger E. *Brethren Social Policy, 1908–1958.* See **14.7.**

4   SCHNEIDER, Herbert Wallace. *Religion in 20th Century America.* Cambridge, Mass., 1952.†

5   SMITH, James W. and A. Leland JAMISON, eds. *Religion in American Life.* 4 vols. Princeton, 1961.

6   SPERRY, Willard L. *Religion in America.* Cambridge, Mass., 1946.†

7   STELZLE, Charles. *American Social and Religious Conditions.* See **14.9.**

8   SWEET, William Warren. *The Story of Religion in America.* Rev. ed. New York, 1950.

9   WILLIAMS, Michael. *American Catholics in the War.* See **25.7.**

10 WISBEY, Herbert A., Jr. *Soldiers Without Swords: A History of the Salvation Army in the United States.* New York, 1955.

6. The Arts

11 BARKER, Virgil. *American Painting, History and Interpretation.* New York, 1950.

12 BOGAN, Louise. *Achievement in American Poetry, 1900–1950.* Chicago, 1951.†

13 BROOKS, Van Wyck. *The Confident Years, 1885–1915.* New York, 1952.

14 BROOKS, Van Wyck. *New England: Indian Summer.* New York, 1940.

15 CHASE, Gilbert. *America's Music.* Rev. ed. New York, 1966.

16 CONDIT, Carl W. *American Building Art.* 2 vols. New York, 1960–1961.

17 CONDIT, Carl W. *The Rise of the Skyscraper.* Chicago, 1952.

18 CULSHAW, John. *A Century of Music.* London, 1952.

19 DOWNER, Alan S. *Fifty Years of American Drama, 1900–1950.* Chicago, 1951.†

20 FITCH, James M. *American Building.* Boston, 1948.

21 GEISMAR, Maxwell D. *The Last of the Provincials: The American Novel, 1915–1925.* Boston, 1947.†

22 GEISMAR, Maxwell D. *Rebels and Ancestors: The Modern American Novel, 1890–1915.* Boston, 1953.†

23 GLICKSBERG, Charles E., ed. *American Literary Criticism, 1900–1950.* New York, 1952.

24 GREGORY, Horace and Marya ZATURENSKA. *A History of American Poetry, 1900–1940.* New York, 1946.

25 GRIFFITH, Linda A. *When the Movies Were Young.* New York, 1925.

26 HICKS, Granville. *The Great Tradition: An Interpretation of American Literature Since the Civil War.* Rev. ed. New York, 1935.

1   HOFFMAN, Frederick J. *The Modern Novel in America, 1900–1950.* Chicago, 1951.†

2   HOWARD, John Tasker. *Our American Music.* Rev. ed. New York, 1946.

3   HOWARD, John Tasker. *Our Contemporary Composers.* New York, 1941.

4   HOWARD, Leon. *Literature and the American Tradition.* Garden City, N.Y., 1960.†

5   KAZIN, Alfred. *On Native Grounds: An Interpretation of Modern American Prose Literature.* New York, 1942.†

6   LARKIN, Oliver W. *Art and Life in America.* New York, 1949.

7   O'CONNOR, William Van. *An Age of Criticism, 1900–1950.* Chicago, 1952.†

8   PHELPS, William Lyon. *The Twentieth Century Theatre.* New York, 1918.

9   RIDEOUT, Walter B. *The Radical Novel in the United States, 1900–1954.* Cambridge, Mass., 1956.†

10 SCHNEIDER, Robert W. *Five Novelists of the Progressive Era.* New York, 1965.

11 SINCLAIR, Upton. *Autobiography.* See **14.17**.

12 SPAETH, Sigmund G. *A History of Popular Music in America.* New York, 1948.

13 SPILLER, Robert E., *et al.,* eds. *Literary History of the United States.* See **2.4**.

14 TAYLOR, Walter F. *The Economic Novel in America.* Chapel Hill, 1942.

15 THORP, Willard. *American Writing in the Twentieth Century.* Cambridge, Mass., 1960.

16 WRIGHT, Frank Lloyd. *An Autobiography.* London, 1932.

17 WRIGHT, Frank Lloyd. *Modern Architecture.* Princeton, 1931.

7. *Journalism*

18 BAKER, Ray Stannard. *American Chronicle.* See **4.3**.

19 BANNISTER, Robert C., Jr. *Ray Stannard Baker.* See **4.6**.

20 BAUMGARTNER, Apollinaris W. *Catholic Journalism: A Study of Its Development in the U.S., 1789–1930.* New York, 1931.

21 BLEYER, Willard G. *Main Currents in the History of American Journalism.* Boston, 1927.

22 BRITT, George. *Forty Years–Forty Millions: The Career of Frank A. Munsey.* New York, 1935.

23 COCHRAN, Negley D. *E. W. Scripps.* New York, 1933.

24 CREEL, George. *Rebel at Large.* See **4.24**.

25 DABNEY, Thomas E. *One Hundred Great Years: The Story of the Times-Picayune From Its Founding to 1940.* Baton Rouge, 1944.

26 DANIELS, Josephus. *Editor in Politics.* See **5.3**.

27 DANIELS, Josephus. *Tar Heel Editor.* See **5.4**.

28 ELLIS, Elmer. *Mr. Dooley's America.* See **5.6**.

1   HEATON, John L. *Cobb of "The World."* New York, 1924.

2   JOHNSON, Walter. *William Allen White's America.* See 6.12.

3   LYON, Peter. *Success Story.* See 14.12.

4   MORRISON, Joseph L. *Josephus Daniels Says. . . . : An Editor's Political Odyssey from Bryan to Wilson and F.D.R., 1894–1913.* Chapel Hill, 1962.

5   MOTT, Frank L. *American Journalism.* See 14.13.

6   MOTT, Frank L. *A History of American Magazines.* See 14.14.

7   NEVINS, Allan. *The Letters and Journal of Brand Whitlock.* See 7.10.

8   NOBLE, David W. "The New Republic and the Idea of Progress, 1914–1920." See 16.12.

9   OLDER, Fremont. *William Randolph Hearst.* See 7.12.

10 PETERSON, Theodore. *Magazines in the Twentieth Century.* Urbana, Ill., 1956.

11 STEFFENS, Lincoln. *The Autobiography of Lincoln Steffens.* See 8.1.

12 SULLIVAN, Mark. *The Education of an American.* See 8.4.

13 SWANBERG, W. A. *Citizen Hearst.* See 8.5.

14 SWANBERG, W. A. *Pulitzer.* See 8.6.

15 THORNBROUGH, Emma Lou. "American Negro Newspapers, 1880–1914." *Bus Hist Rev,* XL (1966), 467-490.

16 VILLARD, Oswald Garrison. *Fighting Years.* See 8.8.

17 WATTERSON, Henry. *"Marse Henry."* See 8.13.

18 WHITE, William Allen. *The Autobiography of William Allen White.* See 8.14.

19 WINTER, Ella and Granville HICKS, eds. *The Letters of Lincoln Steffens.* See 8.15.

20 WITTKE, Carl. *The German-Language Press in America.* See 56.8.

21 WOOD, James P. *Magazines in the United States.* New York, 1949.

8. The Negro

22 BLUMENTHAL, Henry. "Woodrow Wilson and the Race Question." See 20.17.

23 BRODERICK, Francis L. *W. E. B. Du Bois.* See 4.15.

24 BUNI, Andrew. *The Negro in Virginia Politics, 1902–1965.* Charlottesville, Va., 1967.

25 Chicago Commission on Race Relations. *The Negro in Chicago.* See 22.18.

26 EDMONDS, Helen G. *The Negro and Fusion Politics in North Carolina, 1894–1901.* Chapel Hill, 1951.

27 FRANKLIN, John Hope. *From Slavery to Freedom.* See 2.19.

28 FRAZIER, E. Franklin. *The Negro Family in the United States.* Chicago, 1939.

29 GREENE, Lorenzo J. and Carter G. WOODSON. *The Negro Wager Earner.* Washington, D.C., 1930.

1   HARLAN, Louis R. *Separate and Unequal: Public School Campaigns and Racism in the Southern Seaboard States, 1901–1915.* Chapel Hill, 1958.

2   JACK, Robert L. *History of the National Association for the Advancement of Colored People.* See **9.11**.

3   JOHNSON, Charles S. *Patterns of Negro Segregation.* New York, 1943.

4   JOHNSON, Guion Griffis. "The Ideology of White Supremacy, 1876–1910." *Essays in Southern History Presented to Joseph Gregoire de Roulhac Hamilton. . . .* Ed. by Fletcher M. Green. Chapel Hill, 1949.

5   KELLOGG, Charles Flint. *NAACP.* See **9.12**.

6   KENNEDY, Louise V. *The Negro Peasant Turns Cityward.* See **44.7**.

7   LOGAN, Rayford W. *The Negro in American Life and Thought: The Nadir, 1877–1901.* New York, 1954.†

8   MANDEL, Bernard. "Samuel Gompers and the Negro Worker, 1886–1914." See **53.4**.

9   MEIER, August. *Negro Thought in America, 1880–1915.* Ann Arbor, Mich., 1963.

10 MEIER, August. "The Rise of Segregation in the Federal Bureaucracy, 1900–1930." *Phylon,* XXVIII (1967), 178-184.

11 MEIER, August. "Toward a Reinterpretation of Booker T. Washington." *J S Hist,* XXIII (1957), 220-227.

12 MEIER, August and Elliot M. RUDWICK. *From Plantation to Ghetto.* New York, 1966.

13 MYRDAL, Gunnar. *An American Dilemma.* 2 vols. New York, 1944.†

14 NEWBY, I. A. *Jim Crow's Defense: Anti-Negro Thought in America, 1900–1930.* Baton Rouge, 1965.

15 REID, Ira DeA. *The Negro Immigrant.* New York, 1939.

16 ROSS, Frank A. and Louise V. KENNEDY. *A Bibliography of Negro Migration.* New York, 1934.

17 RUDWICK, Elliott M. *Race Riot at East St. Louis, July 2, 1917.* See **24.14**.

18 RUDWICK, Elliott M. *W. E. B. Du Bois: A Study in Minority Group Leadership.* Philadelphia, 1960.

19 SCHEINER, Seth M. *Negro Mecca: A History of the Negro in New York City, 1865–1920.* New York, 1965.

20 SCHEINER, Seth M. "President Theodore Roosevelt and the Negro, 1901–1908." See **18.7**.

21 SCOTT, Emmet J. *Negro Migration during the War.* New York, 1920.

22 SCROGGS, William O. "Interstate Migration of Negro Population." *J Pol Econ,* XXV (1917), 1034-1043.

23 SMITH, T. Lynn. "The Redistribution of the Negro Population in the United States, 1910–1960." *J Neg Hist,* LI (1966), 155-173.

24 SPEAR, Allan H. *Black Chicago: The Making of a Negro Ghetto, 1890–1920.* Chicago, 1967.

25 SPENCER, Samuel R., Jr. *Booker T. Washington and the Negro's Place in American Life.* Boston, 1955.†

1   SPERO, Sterling D. and Abram L. HARRIS. *The Black Worker.* New York, 1931.

2   THORNBROUGH, Emma Lou. "American Negro Newspapers, 1880–1914." See **63.15**.

3   WASHINGTON, Booker T. *Up From Slavery.* See **8.12**.

4   WESLEY, Charles H. *Negro Labor in the United States.* New York, 1927.

5   WHITE, Walter. *Rope & Faggot.* New York, 1929.

6   WILLARD, George-Anne. "Charles Lee Coon: Negro Education and the Atlanta Speech Controversy." *East Carolina College Publications in History,* III (1966), 151-174.

7   WISH, Harvey. "Negro Education and the Progressive Movement." *J Neg Hist,* XLIX (1964), 184-200.

8   WOLGEMUTH, Kathleen Long. "Woodrow Wilson's Appointment Policy and the Negro." See **22.4**.

9   WOODWARD, C. Vann. *Origins of the New South, 1877–1913.* See **12.8**.

10 WOODWARD, C. Vann. *The Strange Career of Jim Crow.* Rev. ed. New York, 1966.†

11 WOOFTER, Thomas J. *Negro Migration: Changes in Rural Organization and Population of the Cotton Belt.* New York, 1920.

12 WYNES, Charles P. *Forgotten Voices: Dissenting Southerners in an Age of Conformity.* Baton Rouge, 1967.

9. Nativism

13 ALEXANDER, Charles C. *The Ku Klux Klan in the Southwest.* Lexington, Ky., 1965.†

14 ALLPORT, Gordon W. *The Nature of Prejudice.* Boston, 1954.†

15 AVIN, Benjamin H. "The Ku Klux Klan, 1915–1925: A Study in Religious Intolerance." Doctoral dissertation, Georgetown University, 1952.

16 BERTHOFF, Rowland T. "Southern Attitudes Toward Immigration, 1865–1914." See **54.22**.

17 BLUM, John M. "Nativism, Anti-Radicalism, and the Foreign Scare, 1917–1920." See **22.13**.

18 BOWERS, David F., ed. *Foreign Influences in American Life.* See **54.23**.

19 CHAFEE, Zechariah, Jr. *Free Speech in the United States.* See **22.17**.

20 CHALMERS, David Mark. *Hooded Americanism: The First Century of the Ku Klux Klan, 1865–1965.* Garden City, N.Y., 1965.

21 CLAGHORN, Kate Hollady. *The Immigrant's Day in Court.* New York, 1923.

22 COBEN, Stanley. *A. Mitchell Palmer.* See **4.19**.

23 COBEN, Stanley. "A Study in Nativism: The American Red Scare of 1919–1920." See **22.22**.

24 CURTI, Merle E. *The Roots of American Loyalty.* See **23.5**.

25 DANIELS, Roger. *The Politics of Prejudice.* See **34.16**.

26 FAIRCHILD, Henry Pratt. "The Literacy Test and Its Making." See **55.4**.

1   GARIS, Roy L. *Immigration Restriction*. See **55.6**.

2   GOSSETT, Thomas F. *Race: The History of an Idea in America*. Dallas, 1963.†

3   HANDLIN, Oscar. "American Views of the Jew at the Opening of the Twentieth Century." See **55.9**.

4   HANDLIN, Oscar. *Race and Nationality in American Life*. See **55.10**.

5   HANSEN, Marcus L. *The Immigrant in American History*. See **55.12**.

6   HARTMANN, Edward George. *The Movement to Americanize the Immigrant*. New York, 1948.

7   HIGHAM, John. *Strangers in the Land*. See **3.6**.

8   ICHIHASHI, Yamato. *Japanese in the United States*. See **55.17**.

9   JACKSON, Kenneth T. *The Ku Klux Klan in the City, 1915–1930*. New York, 1967.

10   JENKS, Jeremiah W. and W. Jett LAUCK. *The Immigrant Problem*. See **55.18**.

11   JOHNSON, Donald D. *The Challenge to American Freedoms*. See **23.15**.

12   KINZER, Donald E. *An Episode in Anti-Catholicism: The American Protective Association*. Seattle, 1964.

13   KOHLER, Max. *Immigration and Aliens in the United States*. New York, 1936.

14   LOUCKS, Emerson Hunsberger. *The Ku Klux Klan in Pennsylvania: A Study in Nativism*. Harrisburg, Pa., 1936.

15   MATTHEWS, Fred H. "White Community and 'Yellow Peril.' " See **55.22**.

16   MC WILLIAMS, Carey. *A Mask for Privilege: Anti-Semitism in America*. Boston, 1948.

17   MECKLIN, John Moffatt. *The Ku Klux Klan: A Study of the American Mind*. New York, 1924.

18   MILLER, Robert M. "A Note of the Relationship between the Protestant Churches and the Ku Klux Klan." *J S Hist*, XXII (1956), 257-266.

19   MILLIS, Harry A. *The Japanese Problem in the United States*. See **55.24**.

20   MURPHY, John C. *An Analysis of the Attitudes of American Catholics Toward the Immigrant and the Negro, 1825–1925*. Washington, D.C., 1940.

21   MURRAY, Robert K. *Red Scare*. See **24.2**.

22   MYERS, Gustavus. *A History of Bigotry in the United States*. New York, 1943.†

23   PRESTON, William, Jr. *Aliens and Dissenters*. See **24.13**.

24   RICE, Arnold S. *The Ku Klux Klan in American Politics*. Washington, D.C., 1962.

25   ROSS, Edward A. *Seventy Years of It*. See **7.23**.

26   SANDMEYER, Elmer C. *The Anti-Chinese Movement in California*. See **35.23**.

27   SAVETH, Edward A. *American Historians and European Immigrants, 1875–1925*. New York, 1948.

1   SCHEIBER, Harry N. *The Wilson Administration and Civil Liberties, 1917–1921.* See **24.15**.

2   STAUFFER, Alvin Packer, Jr. "Anti-Catholicism in American Politics, 1865–1900." Doctoral dissertation, Harvard University, 1931.

3   SWISHER, Carl Brent. "Civil Liberties in War Time." See **24.18**.

4   TANNENBAUM, Frank. *Darker Phases of the South.* New York, 1924.

5   TAYLOR, Joseph Henry. "The Restriction of European Immigration, 1890–1924." See **56.4**.

6   WARTH, Robert D. "The Palmer Raids." See **25.2**.

7   WEAVER, Norman F. "The Knights of the Ku Klux Klan in Wisconsin, Indiana, Ohio, and Michigan." Doctoral dissertation, University of Wisconsin, 1954.

8   WITTKE, Carl. *The German-Americans and the World War.* See **25.9**.

9   WITTKE, Carl. *We Who Built America.* See **56.10**.

NOTES

Index

Aaron, Daniel, 15.20, 57.7
Abell, Aaron I., 13.24, 13.25, 60.2, 60.3, 60.4
Abrams, Ray H., 22.5, 60.1
Abrams, Richard M., 9.23, 9.24, 20.15
Adamic, Louis, 51.1, 54.16, 54.17
Adams, Graham, Jr., 16.16, 51.2
Adams, Henry, 57.8
Addams, Jane, 4.1, 4.2, 12.12, 12.13
Adler, Selig, 22.6, 27.1, 30.10
Agg, Thomas R., 48.14
Aitken, Hugh G. T., 46.19
Alexander, Charles C., 65.13
Allen, Frederick Lewis, 43.4, 45.24, 45.25
Allen, H. C., 32.15
Allen, Howard W., 8.18, 36.12
Allport, Gordon W., 65.14
Ameringer, Charles D., 30.11, 30.12
Anderson, Eugene N., 32.16
Anderson, H. Dewey, 51.3
Anderson, Oscar E., Jr., 16.17
Andrews, John B., 46.20
Armstrong, Maurice W., 60.5
Arnett, Alex Mathews, 22.7
Atherton, Lewis E., 56.12
Auxier, George W., 28.12
Avin, Benjamin H., 65.15

Babcock, Kendric C., 54.18
Baber, Ray Erwin, 56.13
Babson, Roger W., 18.18, 51.4
Bacon, Charles Reade, 9.25
Bagby, Wesley M., 22.8
Bailey, Joseph C., 49.22
Bailey, Kenneth K., 60.6
Bailey, Liberty Hyde, 49.23
Bailey, Thomas A., 27.2, 27.3, 27.4, 28.13, 33.24, 33.25, 34.1, 34.2, 36.13, 36.14, 36.15, 39.11, 39.12, 39.13
Baker, George, 30.13
Baker, O. E., 43.18
Baker, Ray Stannard, 4.3, 4.4, 4.5, 18.19, 18.20, 36.16, 39.14, 62.18
Bannister, Robert C., Jr., 4.6, 62.19
Barger, Harold, 49.24
Baritz, Loren, 46.21
Barker, Charles A., 4.7, 57.9
Barker, John Marshall, 13.26, 60.7
Barker, Virgil, 61.11
Barry, Colman J., 54.19, 60.8
Bartlett, Ruhl J., 39.15
Baruch, Bernard M., 22.9
Bassett, T. D. Seymour, 1.3
Bates, J. Leonard, 14.20, 14.21, 20.16

Baumgartner, Apollinaris W., 62.20
Beale, Howard K., 27.5, 30.14, 32.17, 34.3
Bean, Walton E., 10.1
Beasley, Norman, 7.27, 21.23
Beaver, Daniel R., 22.10, 22.11
Beck, Holmes, 58.1
Bedford, Henry F., 26.14
Beers, Burton F., 34.4, 34.5
Bell, Herbert C. F., 4.8, 18.21
Bemis, Samuel Flagg, 1.4, 27.6, 30.15
Benedict, Murray R., 49.25
Berbusse, Edward J., 30.16
Berger, Harold, 46.22
Berglund, Abraham, 46.23
Berle, Adolf A., 44.12
Berman, Edward, 51.5, 51.6
Bernard, William S., 54.20
Bernstorff, Johann H. von, 36.17
Berthoff, Rowland T., 54.21, 54.22, 65.16
Bethman Hollweg, Theobald von, 36.18
Bidwell, Percy W., 24.21
Billington, Monroe Lee, 4.9, 36.19
Bing, Alexander M., 22.12, 51.7
Birdsall, Paul, 36.20, 39.16
Birnbaum, Karl E., 36.21
Birr, Kendall, 55.2
Blair, John M., 50.21
Blaisdell, Thomas C., Jr., 2.8, 44.13
Blake, Nelson Manfred, 27.7
Bleyer, Willard G., 62.21
Blum, John M., 4.10, 4.11, 7.9, 16.18, 17.21, 18.22, 18.23, 18.24, 22.13, 29.15, 31.21, 35.13, 65.17
Blumberg, Dorothy Rose, 4.12, 12.14
Blumenthal, Henry, 20.17, 63.22
Bogan, Louise, 61.12
Bogart, Ernest Ludlow, 22.14
Bogue, Allan G., 50.1
Bonbright, James C., 44.14, 48.15
Boudin, Louis B., 25.11
Bowers, Claude G., 4.13, 8.19
Bowers, David F., 54.23, 65.18
Braeman, John, 8.20, 16.19
Bragdon, Henry W., 4.14, 19.1
Braisted, William R., 34.6, 34.7, 34.8
Brandeis, Elizabeth, 2.9, 51.8
Brandeis, Louis D., 45.26
Brauer, Jerald C., 60.9
Breckinridge, Sophonisba, 56.14
Bremner, Robert H., 12.15, 12.16, 12.17
Brindley, John E., 48.14
Brissenden, Paul F., 26.15, 51.9, 51.10

Index

Britt, George, **62.22**
Broderick. Francis L., **4.15**, **63.23**
Brody, David, **22.15**, **51.11**, **51.12**
Brooke, Elisabeth W., **56.17**
Brooks, Aubrey L., **4.16**, **8.21**
Brooks, Van Wyck, **61.13**, **61.14**
Bruno, Frank, Jr., **12.18**
Bryan, Mary B., **4.17**, **8.22**, **36.22**
Buchanan, Russell, **36.23**
Buder, Stanley, **51.13**
Buehrig, Edward H., **36.24**, **37.1**, **39.17**
Buell, Raymond L., **34.9**
Buley, R. Carlyle, **46.24**
Bullock, Charles T., **27.8**
Buni, Andrew, **63.24**
Burner, David, **19.2**, **20.18**, **22.16**
Burnett, Philip Mason, **39.18**
Burns, Arthur Robert, **44.15**, **44.16**
Burns, Edward McNall, **58.2**
Burr, Nelson, R., **1.6**
Burton, David H., **28.14**, **28.15**, **32.18**
Busbey, Katherine G., **56.15**
Butler, Nicholas Murray, **58.3**
Butt, Archibald W., **4.18**, **16.20**
Butts, R. Freeman, **58.4**

Callcott, Wilfred A., **30.17**
Calvert, Peter, **30.18**
Cameron, Meribeth E., **34.10**
Campbell, Alexander E., **32.19**
Campbell, Charles S., Jr., **32.20**
Campbell, E. G., **48.16**
Campbell, John P., **32.21**
Cambon, Henri, **37.2**
Cargill, Oscar, **57.10**
Carpenter, Niles, **54.24**
Carstensen, Vernon, **58.10**
Chafee, Zechariah, Jr., **22.17**, **65.19**
Chalmers, David Mark, **14.10**, **65.20**
Chamberlain, John, **2.10**, **8.23**
Chambers, Clarke A., **12.19**
Chaney, Lucian W., **46.25**
Chapin, Robert C., **51.14**
Chase, Gilbert, **61.15**
Child, Clifton J., **37.3**, **54.25**
Churchill, Winston S., **37.4**, **39.19**
Claghorn, Kate Holladay, **65.21**
Clapesattle, Helen, **59.11**
Clark, Earle, **43.19**
Clark, John Bates, **2.11**, **44.17**
Clark, John D., **2.12**, **20.19**, **44.18**
Clark, John Maurice, **2.11**, **22.19**, **44.17**
Clark, Victor S., **47.1**
Clark, Walter E., **45.2**
Clarkson, Grosvenor B., **22.20**

Clay, Howard B., **16.21**
Clemen, Rudolf Alexander, **47.2**
Clendenen, Clarence C., **30.19**
Clews, Henry, **45.27**
Clinard, Outten J., **34.11**
Cline, Howard F., **30.20**
Coben, Stanley, **4.19**, **22.21**, **22.22**, **43.3**, **65.22**, **65.23**
Cochran, Negley D., **62.23**
Cochran, Thomas C., **43.5**, **43.6**, **47.3**
Coffman, Edward M., **39.20**
Cohen, Naomi W., **32.22**
Coit, Margaret L., **4.20**, **22.23**
Cole, Arthur Harrison, **47.4**
Coletta, Paola E., **4.21**, **8.24**, **27.9**, **28.16**, **28.17**, **30.21**, **34.12**
Commager, Henry S., **15.21**, **57.11**
Commons, John R., **4.22**, **55.1**
Condit, Carl W., **6.16**, **61.17**
Coombs, Whitney, **41.15**
Copland, Melvin Thomas, **47.5**
Copley, Frank Barkley, **47.6**
Corey, Lewis, **46.1**
Cornell, Robert J., **16.22**
Corwin, Edward S., **25.12**, **25.13**, **25.14**
Costrell, Edwin, **22.24**
Cramer, Clarence H., **4.23**, **22.25**, **39.21**
Creel, George, **4.24**, **39.22**, **62.24**
Cremin, Lawrence A., **58.4**, **58.5**
Crighton, John C., **23.1**, **37.5**
Croly, Herbert D., **5.1**, **16.23**, **34.13**
Cronin, Bernard J., **51.16**
Cronon, E. David, **5.2**, **19.3**, **19.4**, **37.6**, **39.23**
Crooks, James B., **9.26**
Cross, Whitney R., **14.22**
Crowell, Benedict, **23.2**
Cubberly, Ellwood P., **58.6**, **58.7**
Cuff, Robert D., **23.3**
Culshaw, John, **61.18**
Cumberland, Charles C., **30.22**
Cummins, Cedric C., **23.4**
Current, Richard N., **39.24**
Curry, George, **40.1**
Curry, Roy W., **34.14**, **34.15**
Curti, Merle E., **15.22**, **23.5**, **37.7**, **55.2**, **57.12**, **58.8**, **58.9**, **58.10**, **65.24**
Cushman, Robert E., **2.13**, **44.19**
Cutlip, Scott M., **8.25**

Dabney, Charles William, **58.11**
Dabney, Thomas E., **62.25**
Daniel, Robert L., **32.23**

Index

Daniels, Josephus, **5.3**, **5.4**, **5.5**, **8.26**, **9.1**, **19.5**, **37.8**, **40.2**, **62.26**, **62.27**
Daniels, Roger, 34.16, 55.3, 65.25
Dankof, Ralph H., **47.20**
Darling, Arthur B., **15.1**
Davidson, Elizabeth H., 12.20, 51.17
Davidson, John Wells, 19.6, 20.20
Davidson, Percy E., **51.3**
Davies, George R., **44.2**
Davis, Allen F., **12.21**, **12.22**, **12.23**, **23.6**
Davis, Calvin DeArmond, **32.24**
Davis, G. Cullom, 20.21
Davis, George T., 27.10
Day, Edmund E., **47.7**
Dearing, Charles L., 48.17
De Jouvenel, Bertrand, 19.7
De Kruif, Paul, 59.12
Dennett, Tyler, **28.18**, **33.1**, **34.17**, **34.18**
Dennis, A. L. P., **28.19**, **30.23**, **33.2**, **34.19**
Derber, Milton, **13.1**, **51.18**
Deutsch, Albert, 59.13
Dewing, Arthur S., **44.20**, **46.3**
De Witt, Benjamin Parke, **9.2**
Diamond, Sigmund, **43.7**
Diamond, William, **19.8**
Dietel, Else H., **52.1**
Dimock, Marshall E., **19.9**
Director, Aaron, **51.21**
Dixon, Frank Haigh, 48.18
Dodd, William E., **4.5**, **18.20**
Doherty, Herbert J., Jr., **10.2**
Donahue, Gilbert E., **2.5**
Dorfman, Joseph, **16.1**, **16.2**, **57.13**, **57.14**
Dorsett, Lyle W., **2.14**
Doster, James F., 48.19
Douglas, Paul H., **51.19**, **51.20**, **51.21**
Dowing, Cedric B., **46.2**
Downer, Alan S., **61.19**
Draper, Theodore, 23.7
Dubin, Martin David, **37.9**
Dubofsky, Melvyn, **51.22**
Dulles, Foster Rhea, 27.11, **28.20**, **56.16**
Dunne, Gerald T., **25.15**
Dupree, A. Hunter, 59.14, 59.15
Durand, Edward Dana, 44.21
Duroselle, Jean Baptiste, 27.12

Eastman, Crystal, **13.2**, **51.23**
Eddy, Arthur Jerome, 44.22
Edmonds, Helen G., **63.26**
Edwards, George W., **46.4**

Egbert, Donald D., **26.16**
Ekirch, Arthur A., Jr., **57.15**
Ellis, Elmer, **5.6**, **62.28**
Ellis, John Tracy, **1.7**, **60.10**, **60.11**
Ellis, L. Ethan, 27.13
Ely, Richard T., **5.7**, **9.3**
Epstein, Klaus, 37.10, **40.4**
Epstein, Ralph C., **50.16**
Ershkowitz, Herbert, 27.14
Esthus, Raymond A., **34.20**, **34.21**, **34.22**
Eyre, James E., Jr., **28.21**

Fabela, Isidro, **31.1**
Fabricant, Solomon, **47.8**, **51.24**
Fainsod, Merle, **2.15**, **44.23**
Fairchild, Henry Pratt, **55.4**, **65.26**
Farrell, John T., **28.22**
Faulkner, Harold U., **2.16**, **2.17**, **43.8**, **51.25**
Felt, Jeremy P., **13.3**
Ferguson, Maxwell, 48.20
Ferrell, Henry C., Jr., **10.3**
Ferrell, Robert H., 19.10, **40.5**
Fifield, Russell H., 34.23
Fike, Claude E., **40.6**, **40.7**
Filene, Peter, 27.15
Filler, Louis, 14.11
Fine, Sidney, **2.18**
Finkelstein, Maurice, **25.16**
Fischer, Fritz, 37.11, **40.8**
Fitch, James M., **61.20**
Fite, Gilbert C., **15.10**, **24.11**
Fitzgibbon, Russell H., **31.2**
Fleming, Denna F., **40.9**
Fleming, Donald, 59.16
Flexner, Eleanor, **9.4**
Flexner, J. T., 59.17
Flexner, Simon, 59.17
Flinn, Alfred D., **50.17**
Flint, Winston Allen, **10.4**
Foerster, Robert F., **52.1**, **55.5**
Foner, Philip S., **52.2**
Forcey, Charles, **16.3**
Ford, Worthington C., **57.16**
Fowler, Dorothy, **5.8**, **16.24**
Fox, Daniel M., **16.4**, **57.17**
Frankfurter, Felix, **25.17**, **52.3**
Franklin, John Hope, **2.19**, **63.27**
Frazier, E. Franklin, **63.28**
Freidel, Frank, **5.9**, **19.11**, **40.10**
French, Carroll E., **52.4**
French, John C., **58.12**
Friedman, Milton, **43.9**
Frothingham, Thomas G., **40.11**
Fuller, Joseph V., **31.3**, **34.24**, **37.12**

Index

Furniss, Norman F., **60.12**

Gabriel, Ralph H., **16.5, 57.18**
Galpin, Charles J., **44.1**
Garis, Roy L., **55.6, 66.1**
Garraty, John A., **5.10, 5.11, 5.12, 5.13, 16.25, 19.12, 19.13, 19.14, 25.18, 40.12, 46.5, 47.9, 52.5**
Gaskill, Nelson B., **44.24**
Gatewood, Willard B., **16.26**
Gaus, John M., **50.2**
Gaustad, Edwin Scott, **60.13**
Geiger, Louis G., **5.14, 10.5**
Geismar, Maxwell D., **61.21, 61.22**
Gelber, Lionel M., **33.3**
Gelfand, Lawrence E., **40.13**
George, Alexander L., **5.15, 19.15**
George, Juliette L., **5.15, 19.15**
Gerard, James W., **37.13**
Gerson, Louis L., **40.14**
Gibb, George Sweet, **47.10**
Gillette, John M., **44.2**
Ginger, Ray, **3.1, 5.16, 26.17**
Gini, Corrado, **44.3**
Gist, Genevieve B., **10.6**
Glaab, Charles N., **10.7**
Glad, Paul W., **5.17, 9.5**
Glass, Carter, **20.22, 46.6**
Glazer, Nathan, **60.4**
Glicksberg, Charles E., **61.23**
Gluck, Elsie, **52.6**
Goedecke, Robert, **25.19**
Goldenweiser, Emanuel A., **50.3**
Goldman, Eric F., **16.6, 23.8**
Goldmark, Josephine C., **5.18, 13.4**
Goldsmith, Raymond W., **43.10**
Gompers, Samuel, **5.19, 52.7**
Goodrich, Carter, **44.4**
Gordon, Lincoln, **2.15, 44.23**
Gordon, Milton M., **55.7**
Gossett, Thomas F., **66.2**
Gottfried, Alex, **5.20, 10.8**
Graebner, Norman A., **27.16**
Grantham, Dewey W., Jr., **1.8, 5.21, 9.6, 10.9, 20.23, 40.15**
Graves, William S., **40.16**
Grayson, Cary T., **5.22, 19.16**
Green, Constance, **10.10**
Green, Fletcher M., **10.11**
Green, Marguerite, **3.2, 52.8**
Greene, Fred, **27.17**
Greene, Lorenzo, J., **63.29**
Greene, N., **52.3**
Greenlee, Howard Scott, **19.17**
Greer, Thomas H., **13.5**

Gregory, Charles O., **52.9**
Gregory, Horace, **61.24**
Gregory, Ross, **37.14**
Grenville, John A. S., **27.18**
Grew, Joseph C., **37.15, 40.17**
Grey, Edward, **37.16**
Griffin, Grace Gardner, **1.4**
Griffin, Linda A., **61.25**
Griswold, A. Whitney, **35.1**
Grunder, Garel A., **35.2**
Gulick, Charles A., **3.18, 21.21, 45.18, 46.14**
Gwinn, William Rea, **5.23, 17.1**
Gwynn, Stephen, **33.4, 37.17, 40.18**

Haber, Samuel, **9.7, 47.11**
Hackney, Sheldon, **10.12**
Hagedorn, Hermann, **5.24, 5.25, 17.2, 23.9, 31.4, 37.18, 37.19**
Hall, Frederick S., **56.17**
Hall, Luella J., **33.5**
Hamilton, Walton H., **25.20, 44.25, 50.18**
Hammond, John W., **47.12**
Handlin, Oscar, **1.9, 55.8, 55.9, 55.10, 55.11, 66.3, 66.4**
Handy, Robert T., **26.18, 60.15**
Hanna, Hugh S., **46.25**
Hansen, Alvin H., **52.10, 52.11**
Hansen, Marcus L., **55.12, 55.13, 66.5**
Harbaugh, William H., **6.1, 17.3, 29.1, 31.5, 33.6, 35.3, 37.20**
Harbeson, Robert W., **3.3, 48.21**
Harbison, Winfred A., **25.22**
Harbord, James G., **40.19**
Harding, T. Swann, **50.4**
Hargreaves, Mary Wilma M., **50.5**
Harlan, Louis R., **64.1**
Harrington, Fred H., **29.2, 29.3, 35.4**
Harris, Abram L., **65.1**
Harris, Seymour E., **20.24, 46.7**
Harrow, Benjamin, **59.18**
Hart, Robert A., **27.19**
Hartmann, Edward George, **66.6**
Hartz, Louis, **16.7**
Hawkins, Hugh, **58.13**
Hays, Samuel P., **3.4, 3.5, 10.13, 15.2**
Heald, Morrell, **55.14**
Healy, David F., **31.6**
Heaton, John L., **63.1**
Hechler, Kenneth W., **17.4**
Heckscher, August, **19.18, 19.19**
Heindel, Richard H., **33.7**
Heinrichs, Waldo H., Jr., **37.21**

Helbich, Wolfgang, J., **40**.20
Helmes, Winifred G., **6**.2, **10**.14
Henderson, Gerard C., **45**.1
Hendrick, Burton J., **6**.3, **6**.4, **37**.22, **47**.13, **40**.21
Herberg, Will, **60**.16
Herbst, Jurgen, **58**.14
Herring, George C., Jr., **37**.23
Hicks, Granville, **8**.15, **14**.19, **61**.26, **63**.19
Hicks, John D., **15**.16, **50**.9
Hidy, Muriel E., **47**.14
Hidy, Ralph W., **47**.14
Higham, John, **1**.10, **3**.6, **55**.15, **66**.7
Hill, Forest G., **43**.4
Hill, Joseph A., **52**.12
Hillje, John W., **9**.8
Hillquit, Morris, **26**.19
Himmelberg, Robert F., **23**.10
Hines, Walker D., **23**.11
Hirst, David W., **10**.15, **37**.24
Hoffman, Frederick J., **62**.1
Hofstadter, Richard, **3**.7, **9**.9, **29**.4, **57**.19
Hoglund, A. William, **55**.16
Hohman, Elmo Paul, **20**.25, **52**.13, **52**.14
Holden, Arthur C., **13**.6
Hollingsworth, J. Rogers, **3**.8, **17**.5
Holt, James, **17**.6, **19**.20
Holt, W. Stull, **40**.22, **58**.15
Hook, Sidney, **16**.8, **57**.20, **58**.16
Hoover, Edgar M., Jr., **44**.5, **47**.15
Hoover, Herbert, **40**.23
Hopkins, Charles Howard, **14**.1, **60**.17, **60**.18
Hornig, Edgar Albert, **17**.7
Houston, David F., **6**.5, **19**.21
Hovenstine, E. Jay, Jr., **23**.12
Howard, John Tasker, **62**.2, **62**.3
Howard, Leon, **62**.4
Howe, Frederic C., **6**.6, **9**.10, **13**.7
Howe, M. A. DeWolfe, **6**.7, **17**.8
Hudson, Winthrop S., **60**.19
Huntington-Wilson, F. M., **35**.5
Hurley, Edward N., **23**.13
Hutchins, John G. B., **48**.22
Hutchinson, William T., **6**.8, **19**.22
Huthmacher, J. Joseph, **6**.9, **10**.16, **10**.17

Ichihashi, Yamato, **55**.17, **66**.11
Isaac, Paul E., **10**.18
Ise, John, **21**.1, **47**.16

Jack, Robert L., **9**.11, **64**.2
Jackson, Kenneth T., **66**.8
James, Marquis, **47**.17
Jamieson, Stuart, **15**.11, **50**.6
Jamison, A. Leland, **61**.5
Jamison, Alden, **33**.8
Jenks, Jeremiah Whipple, **45**.2, **55**.18, **66**.9
Jerome, Harry, **44**.6, **50**.19
Jessup, Philip C., **6**.10, **17**.9, **31**.7, **33**.9, **35**.6
Johnson, Allen, **1**.11
Johnson, Arthur M., **17**.10, **45**.3
Johnson, Carolyn W., **17**.11
Johnson, Charles S., **64**.3
Johnson, Donald D., **23**.15, **66**.10
Johnson, Emory R., **43**.11
Johnson, Guion Griffis, **64**.4
Johnson, Stanley C., **55**.19
Johnson, Tom L., **6**.11, **10**.19
Johnson, Walter, **6**.12, **63**.2
Jones, Eliot, **45**.4
Jones, Maldwyn Allen, **55**.20
Joost, Nicholas, **57**.21
Josephson, Matthew, **50**.20

Kahle, Louis G., **3**.18
Kandel, I. L., **58**.17, **58**.18
Kaplan, Louis, **1**.12
Kaplan, Sidney, **23**.16
Karraker, William Archibald, **29**.5
Karson, Marc, **3**.9, **52**.16
Kazin, Alfred, **62**.5
Keir, Malcolm, **47**.18
Keller, Morton, **25**.21, **47**.19
Kellogg, Charles Flint, **9**.12, **64**.5
Kellogg, Paul Underwood, **9**.13, **52**.17
Kelly, Alfred H., **25**.22
Kemble, John Haskell, **48**.23
Kemmerer, Edwin A., **21**.2
Kendrick, John W., **43**.12
Kennan, George, **48**.24
Kennan, George F., **27**.20, **40**.24, **40**.25
Kennedy, Albert J., **13**.22
Kennedy, Edward D., **49**.1
Kennedy, Louise V., **44**.7, **64**.6, **64**.16
Kerney, James, **6**.13, **19**.23
Kerr, James J., **21**.3
Kerr, K. Austin, **23**.17
Kerr, William T., Jr., **10**.20
Kester, Randall B., **23**.18
King, Judson, **15**.3
King, Willard L., **25**.23
King, Willford I., **43**.13, **43**.14

Index

Kinzer, Donald E., **66**.12
Kipnis, Ira A., **26**.20
Kirsh, Benjamin S., **45**.5
Kirwan, Albert D., **10**.21
Klebaner, Benjamin J., **21**.4, **45**.6
Klinkhamer, Marie Carolyn, **25**.24
Knauth, Oswald Whitman, **45**.7
Knight, Edgar W., **58**.19
Knowlton, Evelyn H., **47**.10
Knox, Israel, **60**.20
Kohler, Max, **66**.13
Koistinen, Paul A. C., **23**.19
Kolko, Gabriel, **3**.10, **3**.11, **9**.14, **49**.2
Kraditor, Aileen S., **9**.15
Kube, Harold D., **47**.20
Kuehl, Warren F., **1**.13
Kuhlmann, Charles B., **47**.21
Kutler, Stanley I., **26**.1, **52**.18
Kuznets, Simon, **46**.8

La Follette, Belle C., **6**.14, **17**.12, **19**.24
La Follette, Fola, **6**.14, **17**.12, **19**.24
Lahne, Herbert J., **52**.19
Lambert, John R., **6**.15
Lambert, Oscar D., **6**.16, **17**.13
Lancaster, James L., **40**.26
Landsberg, Hans H., **49**.24
Lane, Anne W., **6**.17, **19**.25
Lanfear, Vincent W., **52**.20
Langer, William L., **37**.25, **40**.27, **41**.1
Lankford, John E., **60**.21
Lansing, Robert, **4**.12, **41**.3
Larkin, Oliver W., **62**.6
Larsen, William, **6**.18, **10**.22
Larson, Cedric, **23**.25
Larson, Henrietta M., **1**.14, **47**.22
Lasch, Christopher, **16**.9, **29**.6, **41**.4, **41**.5
Lasswell, Harold D., **23**.20
Latham, Earl, **19**.26
Latimer, Murray W., **52**.21
Lauck, W. Jett, **52**.22, **55**.18, **66**.9
Laughlin, J. Laurence, **21**.5, **46**.9
Layman, Martha E., **38**.11
Leary, William M., Jr., **21**.6
Lefler, Hugh T., **4**.16, **8**.21
Leiby, James, **52**.23
Leigh, Robert D., **59**.19
Leiserson, William M., **55**.21
Leopold, Richard W., **6**.19, **17**.14, **27**.21, **28**.1, **28**.2, **31**.9, **33**.10, **35**.7, **37**.26
Lerner, Max, **26**.2
Lescohier, Don D., **3**.12, **52**.24, **52**.25
Leuchtenburg, William E., **23**.21, **29**.7

Levin, N. Gordon, Jr., **41**.6
Levine, Daniel, **9**.16, **13**.8, **52**.26
Levine, Lawrence W., **6**.20, **23**.22
Lewis, Cleona, **28**.3
Li, Tien-yi, **35**.8
Lieberman, Elias, **52**.27
Link, Arthur S., **1**.16, **3**.13, **6**.21, **6**.22, **6**.23, **6**.24, **6**.25, **6**.26, **6**.27, **10**.23, **17**.5, **19**.27, **19**.28, **20**.1, **20**.2, **20**.3, **21**.7, **21**.8, **21**.9, **21**.10, **21**.11, **21**.12, **21**.13, **31**.10, **31**.11, **31**.12, **31**.13, **31**.14, **35**.9, **38**.1, **38**.2, **38**.3, **38**.4, **38**.5, **41**.7
Linn, James Weber, **6**.28, **13**.9
Livermore, Seward W., **23**.23, **23**.24, **31**.15, **31**.16, **35**.10
Livezey, William E., **28**.4, **35**.2
Lloyd George, David, **38**.6, **41**.8
Locklin, D. Philip, **49**.3
Lockmiller, David A., **31**.17
Logan, Rayford W., **41**.9, **64**.7
Lombardi, John, **53**.1
Loos, John L., **47**.23
Lord, Walter, **56**.18
Lorwin, Lewis L., **50**.21, **53**.2
Lou, Herbert H., **56**.19
Loucks, Emerson Hunsberger, **66**.14
Louis, William Roger, **41**.10
Lowitt, Richard, **7**.1, **10**.24, **15**.4, **17**.16, **38**.7, **49**.4.
Lowry, Bullitt, **41**.11
Lubove, Roy, **13**.10, **13**.11, **13**.12, **13**.13, **13**.14, **13**.15.
Lyon, Peter, **14**.12, **63**.3

McAdoo, William G., **7**.6, **20**.4
McAvoy, Thomas T., **60**.24
McCloskey, Robert Green, **57**.23
McCormick, Thomas J., **29**.10, **35**.11
McDonald, Forrest, **47**.24, **47**.25
McGann, Thomas F., **31**.18
McGeary, M. Nelson, **7**.7, **15**.5, **17**.18
McGovern, George S., **21**.14
McGovern, James R., **56**.22
McKee, Delber L., **29**.11
McKelvey, Blake, **11**.4
McLaughlin, Glenn E., **47**.26
McReynolds, George E., **36**.1
McWilliams, Carey, **66**.16
Madison, Charles A., **9**.17
Malone, Dumas, **1**.11
Mamatey, Victor S., **41**.12
Mandel, Bernard, **7**.2, **53**.3, **53**.4, **64**.8
Mangold, George B., **56**.20
Mann, Arthur, **7**.3, **11**.1, **16**.10
Manny, Theodore B., **44**.1

Mantoux, Paul, **41.13**
Martin, Laurence W., **41.14, 41.15**
Mason, Alpheus T., **7.4, 9.18, 11.21, 16.11, 17.17, 26.3, 49.17, 53.5**
Mason, Edward S., **49.5**
Matthews, Fred H., **55.22, 66.15**
Maxwell, Kenneth R., **41.16**
Maxwell, Robert S., **7.5, 11.2, 11.3**
May, Ernest R., **1.17, 29.8, 29.9, 38.8, 38.9**
May, Henry F., **14.2, 56.21, 57.22, 60.22**
Mayer, Arno J., **41.17, 41.18**
Maynard, Theodore, **60.23**
Mead, Edward Sherwood, **45.8**
Means, Gardiner C., **44.12, 44.14**
Mecklin, John Moffatt, **66.17**
Meier, August, **64.9, 64.10, 64.11, 64.12**
Merritt, Richard L., **41.19**
Meyer, Balthasar Henry, **17.19, 45.9**
Miller, David Hunter, **41.20**
Miller, Elizabeth W., **1.18**
Miller, Herbert A., **55.23, 55.25**
Miller, Robert Moats, **14.3, 60.25, 66.18**
Miller, Sidney L., **49.6**
Miller, William D., **11.5, 43.6**
Miller, Zane L., **11.6**
Millis, Harry A., **55.24, 66.19**
Millis, Walter, **38.10**
Mills, Frederick C., **3.14, 45.10**
Mims, Edwin, **58.20**
Miner, Dwight C., **31.19**
Minger, Ralph Eldin, **31.20, 35.12**
Mitchell, Wesley C., **3.15, 43.15, 45.11**
Mock, James R., **23.25, 23.26**
Moody, John, **45.12, 46.10**
Mooney, Chase C., **38.11**
Moore, Charles W., **48.1**
Moore, Ernest Carroll, **58.21**
More, Louise B., **53.6**
Morgan, H. Wayne, **26.21, 26.22, 29.12, 29.13, 29.14**
Morison, Elting E., **7.8, 7.9, 17.20, 17.21, 29.15, 31.21, 35.13, 41.21**
Morison, Samuel E., **58.22**
Morlan, Robert L., **15.12**
Morris, Lloyd R., **56.23**
Morris, Richard B., **1.19**
Morrison, Joseph L., **63.4**
Morrissey, Alice, **38.12**
Mott, Frank L., **14.13, 14.14, 63.5, 63.6**
Mott, Rodney L., **26.4**
Mott, T. Bentley, **41.22**

Moulton, Harold G., **45.13, 49.7, 49.8**
Mowry, George E., **1.20, 11.7, 11.8, 17.22, 17.23**
Moynihan, James H., **60.26**
Mullendore, William C., **24.1**
Muller, Dorothea R., **14.4**
Munro, Dana G., **31.22, 31.23, 31.24**
Murphy, John C., **66.20**
Murray, Robert K., **21.15, 24.2, 24.3, 53.7, 66.21**
Myers, Gustavus, **66.22**
Myers, Margaret G., **46.11**
Myrdal, Gunnar, **64.13**

Nadworthy, Milton J., **53.8**
Nash, Gerald D., **24.4, 53.9**
Neale, R. G., **29.16**
Nelson, Milton Nels, **45.15**
Neu, Charles E., **35.14, 35.15**
Neufeld, Maurice F., **2.2**
Nevins, Allan, **7.10, 33.11, 48.2, 49.9, 63.7**
Newby, I. A., **24.5, 64.14**
Newcomer, Mabel, **48.3**
Nicholas, Herbert G., **20.5**
Nicolson, Harold, **41.23**
Noble, David W., **16.12, 16.13, 63.8**
Noble, Ransom E., Jr., **11.9**
Noble, Stuart G., **58.23**
Norris, George W., **7.11, 11.10**
Notter, Harley, **38.13**
Nourse, Edwin G., **50.7**
Noyes, Alexander D., **24.6, 46.12, 46.13**
Nye, Russel B., **11.11**

O'Connor, Harvey, **48.4**
O'Connor, William Van, **62.7**
Odegard, Peter H., **9.19**
O'Gara, Gordon C., **17.24**
O'Grady, Joseph P., **41.24**
Olcott, Charles S., **29.17**
Older, Fremont, **7.12, 63.9**
Oliver, John W., **50.22**
Olmstead, Clifton E., **60.27**
O'Neill, William L., **57.1, 57.2**
Orr, Oliver H., Jr., **7.13, 11.12**
Osborn, George C., **7.14, 11.13**
Osburn, W. J., **59.1**
Osgood, Robert E., **28.5, 41.25**
Ostrander, Gilman Marston, **11.14**

Palmer, Frederick, **7.15, 24.7, 38.14, 41.26, 41.27**
Park, Robert E., **55.25**

Index

Patrick, Rembert W., 1.16
Patterson, Thomas G., 28.6
Paxson, Frederic L., 20.6, 24.8, 24.9, 24.10
Peffer, E. Louise, 15.6
Pelling, Henry, 53.10
Penick, James, Jr., 15.7, 17.25
Perkins, Bradford, 33.12
Perkins, Dexter, 7.16, 21.16, 26.5, 31.25, 42.1
Perlman, Mark, 53.11
Perlman, Selig, 3.16, 53.12, 53.13
Perry, Ralph Barton, 57.24
Pershing, John J., 42.2, 42.3
Persons, Stow, 26.16
Peterson, Horace C., 24.11, 24.12
Peterson, Theodore, 63.10
Phelps, William Lyon, 62.8
Pierson, George Wilson, 59.2
Pike, Frederick B., 31.26
Pinkett, Harold T., 17.26
Pitkin, William A., 17.27
Poincaré, Raymond, 38.15, 42.4
Potter, David M., 57.3
Porter, Eugene, 21.17
Porter, Kenneth Wiggins, 47.22
Potts, E. Daniel, 11.15
Pratt, Julius W., 28.7, 29.18, 29.19, 29.20, 32.1, 35.16, 38.16, 42.5
Prescott, Francis C., 35.17
Preston, William, Jr., 24.13, 66.23
Pringle, Henry F., 7.17, 7.18, 17.28, 18.1, 32.2, 32.3, 33.13, 33.14, 35.18, 35.19
Puleston, William D., 29.21
Pusey, Merlo J., 7.19, 11.16, 21.18, 26.6
Pyle, Joseph G., 49.10

Quint, Howard H., 26.23, 29.22
Quirk, Robert E., 32.4, 32.5

Rappaport, Armin, 38.17
Ratner, Sidney, 3.17, 21.19, 45.16
Rauschenbush, Walter, 14.5, 14.6, 61.1, 61.2
Rayback, Joseph G., 53.14
Read, James Morgan, 38.18
Reed, Louis S., 53.15
Rees, Albert, 53.16
Regier, Cornelius C., 14.15
Reid, Ira DeA., 64.15
Reinsch, Paul S., 35.20
Remer, C. F., 35.21
Reuter, Frank T., 29.33
Reynolds, George M., 11.17

Rice, Arnold S., 66.24
Richardson, Elmo R., 15.8
Rideout, Walter B., 62.9
Ripley, William Z., 18.2, 49.11, 49.12
Rippy, J. Fred, 32.6, 32.7
Ritter, Gerhard, 38.19, 42.6
Robbins, Roy M., 15.9
Roberts, Henry L., 2.3
Roberts, Mary M., 59.20
Roche, John P., 26.7
Rodgers, Andrew Denny, III, 59.21
Roelofs, Vernon W., 26.8
Roosevelt, Theodore, 7.20, 18.3, 32.8, 33.15, 35.22,
Roper, Daniel C., 7.22, 20.7
Ross, Edward A., 7.23, 13.16, 56.13, 66.25
Ross, Frank A., 64.16
Rossi, Alice S., 59.3
Rossi, Peter H., 59.3
Rossiter, William S., 44.8
Rothstein, Morton, 33.16
Rublee, George, 21.22
Rudin, Harry R., 42.7
Rudwick, Elliot M., 24.14, 64.12, 64.17, 64.18
Rugg, Harold, 59.4
Rumble, Wilfred E., Jr., 26.9

Sage, Leland L., 7.24, 18.5
Saloutos, Theodore, 15.13, 15.14, 15.15, 15.16, 50.8, 50.9, 55.26, 56.1
Sandmeyer, Elmer C., 35.23, 66.26
Sappington, Roger E., 14.7, 61.3
Saveth, Edward A., 66.27
Saxton, Alexander, 11.18, 53.17
Scheiber, Harry N., 24.15, 67.1
Scheinberg, Stephen J., 18.6, 53.18
Scheiner, Seth M., 18.7, 64.19, 64.20
Schieber, Clara E., 33.17
Schilpp, Paul Arthur, 59.5
Schluter, William C., 45.17
Schmitt, Bernadotte E., 38.20
Schneider, Herbert W., 57.25
Schneider, Robert Wallace, 6.14, 62.10
Schultz, Stanley K., 14.16
Schurr, Sam H., 46.22
Schwartz, Anna Jacobson, 43.9
Scott, Emmet J., 64.21
Scott, James Brown, 32.9, 33.18, 33.19, 35.24
Scott, Roy V., 49.13
Scroggs, William O., 64.22
Seager, Henry R., 3.18, 21.21, 45.18, 46.14

Index

Sears, Louis Martin, 29.24
Seidman, Joel, 53.19
Selekman, Ben M., 53.20
Sellers, James Brown, 11.19
Seltzer, Lawrence H., 49.14
Severson, Robert F., Jr. 48.5
Seymour, Charles, 7.25, 20.8, 20.9, 38.21, 38.22, 42.8, 42.9
Shannon, David A., 26.24, 26.25
Shannon, Fred A., 15.17, 50.10
Sharfman, I. L., 3.19, 21.22, 45.19, 49.15, 49.16
Shepardson, Whitney H., 50.11
Sherman, Richard B., 11.20
Shippee, Lester B., 30.1, 30.2
Shryock, Richard H., 59.22, 59.23
Silk, Leonard S., 50.23
Simkins, Francis B., 7.26, 15.18
Sims, William S., 42.10
Sinclair, Upton, 14.17, 62.11
Siney, Marion, 38.23, 38.24
Sizer, Theodore R., 59.6
Slosson, Preston W., 24.16
Smith, Daniel M., 24.17, 38.25, 38.26, 38.27
Smith, Darrell Hevenor, 53.21
Smith, James W., 61.5
Smith, John S., 20.10, 53.22
Smith, Rixey, 7.27, 21.23
Smith, T. Lynn, 64.23
Smith, Willard H., 14.8
Smith, William Carlson, 56.2
Smuts, Robert W., 57.4
Snell, John L., 42.11, 42.12
Solvick, Stanley D., 18.8
Soule, George, 43.16
Spaeth, Sigmund G., 62.12
Spargo, John, 42.13
Spear, Allan H., 64.24
Spencer, Samuel R., Jr., 64.25
Spero, Sterling D., 65.1
Sperry, Willard L., 61.6
Spiller, Robert E., 2.4, 62.13
Spindler, Arno, 39.1
Sprague, O. M. W., 46.15
Sprout, Harold, 28.8
Sprout, Margaret, 28.8
Squires, James Duane, 39.2
Staples, Henry L., 11.21, 49.17
Starr, Mark, 51.25
Startt, James D., 42.14
Stauffer, Alvin Packer, Jr., 67.2
Steelman, Joseph F., 11.22, 11.23, 18.9
Steelman, Lala Carr, 13.17, 35.25
Steffens, Lincoln, 8.1, 11.24, 11.25, 14.18, 63.11

Steigerwalt, Albert K., 48.6, 48.7
Stelzle, Charles, 14.9, 61.7
Stephenson, George M., 8.2, 11.26, 32.10, 56.3
Stephenson, Nathaniel W., 8.3, 18.10
Stevens, William H. S., 45.20
Stewart, Bryce M., 53.23
Stewart, Frank M., 11.27
Stigler, George J., 57.5
Stone, Ralph A., 42.15
Strakhovsky, Leonid I., 42.16
Stroud, Gene S., 2.5
Stuart, Graham H., 28.9
Suffern, Arthur E., 53.24
Sullivan, Mark, 3.20, 8.4, 63.12
Sutton, Walter A., 39.3
Swanberg, W. A., 8.5, 8.6, 30.3, 30.4, 63.13, 63.14
Sward, Keith T., 49.18
Sweet, William Warren, 61.8
Swisher, Carl Brent, 24.18, 24.19, 67.3
Sydenstricker, Edgar, 52.22
Syrett, Harold C., 39.4

Taft, Philip, 3.16, 24.20, 53.13, 53.25, 53.26, 54.1, 54.2
Tager, Jack, 9.20
Tannenbaum, Frank, 67.4
Tansill, Charles C., 32.11
Tarbell, Ida M., 48.8
Tate, Merze, 35.26
Taussig, Frank W., 3.21, 21.24
Taylor, A. Elizabeth, 12.1
Taylor, Albion Guilford, 54.3
Taylor, Joseph Henry, 56.4, 67.5
Taylor, Walter F., 62.14
Temperley, H. W. V., 42.17
Thelen, David P., 12.2
Thomas, William I., 56.5, 57.6
Thomas, Woodlief, 47.7
Thompson, Carl W., 50.12
Thompson, Clarence B., 48.9
Thompson, John M., 42.18
Thompson, Tracy E., 48.10
Thompson, Warren S., 44.9
Thorelli, Hans B., 3.22, 45.21
Thornbrough, Emma Lou, 18.11, 63.15, 65.2
Thornthwaite, C. Warren, 44.10
Thorp, Willard L., 48.11, 62.15
Thorson, Winston S., 33.20, 35.27
Thurber, Evangeline, 23.26
Tillman, Seth P., 42.19
Timberlake, James H., 9.21
Tindall, George Brown, 3.23, 20.11
Tinsley, James A., 12.3, 18.12
Tirpitz, Alfred von, 39.5

Index

Tobey, James A., **59**.24
Tobin, Harold J., **24**.21
Todd, A. L., **21**.25, **26**.10
Tolman, William H., **54**.4
Tompkins, E. Berkeley, **30**.5
Towley, Louis, **12**.18
Trask, David F., **42**.20
Trattner, Walter I., **24**.22
Treat, Payson J., **35**.28
True, Alfred C., **50**.13, **50**.14
Truesdale, Leon E., **50**.3, **50**.15
Tupper, Eleanor, **36**.1
Turlington, Edgar, **24**.23, **32**.12,
Twiss, Benjamin R., **26**.11
Tyler, Robert L., **54**.5

Unterberger, Betty M., **42**.21, **42**.22
Urofsky, Melvin I., **21**.26

Vagts, Alfred, **33**.21, **33**.22
Van Alstyne, Richard W., **39**.6, **39**.7
Vance, Maurice M., **8**.7, **16**.14
Van Kleeck, Mary, **53**.20
Van Riper, Paul P., **18**.13
Van Tassel, David D., **59**.7
Varg, Paul A., **36**.2, **36**.3, **36**.4, **36**.5
Vecoli, Rudolph, **56**.6
Vevier, Charles, **36**.6, **36**.7
Veysey, Laurence R., **20**.12, **59**.8
Viereck, George Sylvester, **24**.24, **39**.8
Villard, Osward Garrison, **8**.8, **63**.16

Wade, Louise C., **8**.9, **13**.18
Wakstein, Allen M., **54**.6
Wald, Lillian D., **8**.10, **13**.19
Wall, Louise H., **6**.17, **19**.25
Walworth, Arthur, **8**.11, **20**.13, **39**.9,
  42.23
Warburg, Paul M., **22**.1, **22**.2, **46**.16,
  46.17
Ward, Robert D., **25**.1
Warner, Hoyt Landon, **12**.4
Warner, Robert M., **18**.14
Warren, Charles, **26**.12
Warshow, Herman T., **48**.12
Warth, Robert D., **25**.2, **67**.6
Washington, Booker T., **8**.12, **65**.3
Watkins, Gordon S., **25**.3, **54**.7
Watkins, Myron W., **3**.24, **45**.22
Watson, Richard L., Jr., **2**.6
Watterson, Henry, **8**.13, **63**.17
Way, Royal B., **30**.2
Weaver, Norman F., **67**.7
Weinberg, Albert K., **30**.6

Weinstein, Edwin A., **20**.14, **25**.5
Weinstein, James, **12**.5, **25**.6, **26**.26,
  26.27, **39**.10
Weinstein, Sydney, **25**.4
Weintraub, Hyman, **54**.8
Weiss, Nancy Joan, **13**.20
Welles, Sumner, **32**.13
Wesley, Charles H., **65**.4
Wesser, Robert F., **12**.6
Whelpton, P. K., **44**.9, **54**.9
White, John Albert, **36**.8, **36**.9
White, Morton, **16**.15, **57**.26
White, Walter, **65**.5
White, William Allen, **8**.14, **63**.18
Whiteman, Harold B., Jr., **42**.24
Whitener, Daniel Jay, **12**.7
Wiebe, Robert H., **3**.25, **9**.22, **18**.15,
  18.16
Wilcox, Clair, **45**.23
Wilcox, Delos F., **49**.19, **49**.20
Wilensky, Norman M., **18**.17
Wilkerson, Marcus M., **30**.7
Willard, George-Anne, **65**.6
Willcox, Walter F., **44**.11, **56**.7
Williams, Benjamin H., **28**.10
Williams, Michael, **25**.7, **61**.9
Williams, William A., **28**.11, **30**.8
Williamson, Harold F., **43**.17
Willis, Henry Parker, **22**.3, **46**.18
Willoughby, William Franklin, **25**.8
Wilson, Louis R., **59**.9
Wilson, Robert Frost, **23**.2
Wimer, Kurt, **42**.25, **42**.26, **42**.27
Winter, Ella, **8**.15, **14**.19, **63**.19
Wisan, Joseph E., **30**.9
Wisbey, Herbert A., Jr., **61**.10
Wish, Harvey, **65**.7
Witte, Edwin E., **54**.10
Wittke, Carl, **25**.9, **56**.8, **56**.9, **56**.10,
  63.20, **67**.8, **67**.9
Wolcott, Leon O., **50**.2
Wolgemuth, Kathleen Long, **22**.4, **65**.8
Wolman, Leo, **54**.11, **54**.12
Wood, James P., **63**.21
Wood, Norman J., **48**.13
Wood, Stephen B., **13**.21, **26**.13
Woodbury, Robert M., **54**.13
Woods, Robert A., **13**.22
Woodson, Carter G., **63**.29
Woodward, C. Vann, **8**.16, **12**.8, **15**.19,
  65.9, **65**.10
Woofter, Thomas J., **56**.11, **65**.11
Woolbert, Robert Gale, **2**.7
Wreszin, Michael, **25**.10
Wright, Frank Lloyd, **62**.16, **62**.17
Wright, Herbert F., **32**.14, **33**.23,
  36.10

Index

Wright, Philip G., **46**.23
Wynes, Charles P., **65**.12

Yates, Louis A. R., **43**.1
Yellen, Samuel, **54**.14
Yellowitz, Irwin, **12**.9, **54**.15
Yeomans, Henry A., **59**.10
Young, George Berkeley, **27**.18

Zabriskie, Edward H., **36**.11
Zacharewicz, Mary Misaela, **43**.2
Zaturenska, Marya, **61**.24
Zeis, Paul M., **49**.21
Zimmerman, Jane, **13**.23
Zink, Harold, **12**.10
Znaniecki, Florian, **56**.5, **57**.6
Zucker, Norman L., **8**.17, **12**.11